Careers in Focus

Careers in Focus

DESIGN

THIRD EDITION

Ferguson
An imprint of Infobase Publishing

Careers in Focus: Design, Third Edition

Copyright © 2011 by Infobase Publishing

All rights reserved. No part of this book may be reproduced or utilized in any form or by any means, electronic or mechanical, including photocopying, recording, or by any information storage or retrieval systems, without permission in writing from the publisher. For information contact:

Ferguson
An imprint of Infobase Publishing
132 West 31st Street
New York NY 10001

Library of Congress Cataloging-in-Publication Data

Careers in focus. Design. — 3rd ed.
     p. cm.
  Includes bibliographical references and index.
  ISBN-13: 978-0-8160-8024-3 (hardcover : alk. paper)
  ISBN-10: 0-8160-8024-0 (hardcover : alk. paper) 1. Design—Vocational guidance—Juvenile literature.
  NK1172.C37 2010
  745.4023'73—dc22

Ferguson books are available at special discounts when purchased in bulk quantities for businesses, associations, institutions, or sales promotions. Please call our Special Sales Department in New York at (212) 967-8800 or (800) 322-8755.

You can find Ferguson on the World Wide Web at
http://www.infobasepublishing.com

Text design by David Strelecky
Composition by Mary Susan Ryan-Flynn
Cover printed by Art Print Company, Taylor, PA
Book printed and bound by Maple Press, PA
Date printed: November 2010
Printed in the United States of America

10 9 8 7 6 5 4 3 2 1

This book is printed on acid-free paper.

All links and Web addresses were checked and verified to be correct at the time of publication. Because of the dynamic nature of the Web, some addresses and links may have changed since publication and may no longer be valid.

Table of Contents

Introduction

Design is seen in almost every aspect of our lives. The homes we live in, the clothes we wear, the cars we drive, and the chairs we sit in are all produced with the help of designers. Since design is an art form, individuals working in the design field must be creative and imaginative. But unlike fine artists working on a painting or a sculpture, designers' creations must not only be appealing to the senses, but also serve a larger purpose.

There are two major types of design: *structural* and *decorative*. *Structural designers* must take three things into consideration when creating a design: how a product operates, what it will look like, and how it will be made. In other words, structural designers are concerned with function, form, and material. *Decorative designers* are concerned with the appearance of an object, such as a fine piece of silverware. In this case, the product still must be designed to serve a purpose, but it is the decorative elements that make it attractive to customers.

Designers work in almost every industry. *Graphic designers* work on books, magazines, greeting cards, packaging materials, Web sites, and other projects to create a desired visual "look." *Industrial designers* combine technical knowledge with artistic talent to create or improve manufactured products. *Computer and video game designers* combine computer technology with a creative vision to produce entertaining and educational software and games. *Landscape architects* combine beauty and function to plan outdoor areas. This is only a sampling of the wide array of jobs available.

Because of the diverse nature of the design field, there will always be a need for talented designers in the workplace. When the U.S. economy expands and people demand quality products and services, designers will be in high demand. In general, designers with computer skills, training, and good creative instincts will fare the best in the job market. The increased use of computer-aided design equipment requires a high level of technical skill. The U.S. Department of Labor predicts that employment prospects should be especially strong for the following design professionals: architects, exhibit designers, interior designers and decorators, landscape architects, makeup artists, and production designers and art directors.

However, despite promising employment prospects, the field of design is extremely competitive. Many talented individuals are attracted to design jobs because they enable them to use their creative skills in a profitable way. Job seekers can prepare for the competition in the design field by attending technical and design high schools, becoming acquainted and comfortable with computer software and design programs, and working on establishing contacts within various fields to help them land their first job.

The articles in *Careers in Focus: Design* appear in Ferguson's *Encyclopedia of Careers and Vocational Guidance*, but have been updated and revised with the latest information from the U.S. Department of Labor, professional organizations, and other sources.

The following paragraphs detail the sections and features that appear in the book.

The **Quick Facts** section provides a brief summary of the career, including recommended school subjects, personal skills, work environment, minimum educational requirements, salary ranges, certification or licensing requirements, and employment outlook. This section also provides acronyms and identification numbers for the following government classification indexes: the Dictionary of Occupational Titles (DOT), the Guide for Occupational Exploration (GOE), the National Occupational Classification (NOC) Index, and the Occupational Information Network (O*NET)-Standard Occupational Classification System (SOC) index. The DOT, GOE, and O*NET-SOC indexes have been created by the U.S. government; the NOC index is Canada's career classification system. Readers can use the identification numbers listed in the Quick Facts section to access further information about a career. Print editions of the DOT (*Dictionary of Occupational Titles*. Indianapolis, Ind.: JIST Works, 1991) and GOE (*Guide for Occupational Exploration*. Indianapolis, Ind.: JIST Works, 2001) are available at libraries. Electronic versions of the NOC (http://www23.hrdc-drhc.gc.ca) and O*NET-SOC (http://online.onetcenter.org) are available on the Internet. When no DOT, GOE, NOC, or O*NET-SOC numbers are listed, this means that the U.S. Department of Labor or Human Resources and Skills Development Canada have not created a numerical designation for this career. In this instance, you will see the acronym "N/A," or not available.

The **Overview** section is a brief introductory description of the duties and responsibilities involved in this career. Oftentimes, a career may have a variety of job titles. When this is the case, alternative career titles are presented. Employment statistics are also provided, when available. The **History** section describes the history of the particular job as it relates to the overall development of its industry or field. **The Job** describes the primary and secondary duties of the job. **Requirements** discusses high school and postsecondary education and training requirements, any certification or licensing that is necessary, and other personal requirements for success in the job. **Exploring** offers suggestions on how to gain experience in or knowledge of the particular job before making a firm educational and financial commitment. The focus is on what can be done while still in high school (or in the early years of college) to gain a better understanding of the job. The **Employers** section gives an overview of typical places of employment for the job. **Starting Out** discusses the best ways to land that first job, be it through the college career services office, newspaper ads, Internet employment sites, or personal contact. The **Advancement** section describes what kind of career path to expect from the job and how to get there. **Earnings** lists salary ranges and describes the typical fringe benefits. The **Work Environment** section describes the typical surroundings and conditions of employment—whether indoors or outdoors, noisy or quiet, social or independent. Also discussed are typical hours worked, any seasonal fluctuations, and the stresses and strains of the job. The **Outlook** section summarizes the job in terms of the general economy and industry projections. For the most part, Outlook information is obtained from the U.S. Bureau of Labor Statistics and is supplemented by information gathered from professional associations. Job growth terms follow those used in the *Occupational Outlook Handbook*. Growth described as "much faster than the average" means an increase of 21 percent or more. Growth described as "faster than the average" means an increase of 14 to 20 percent. Growth described as "about as fast as the average" means an increase of 7 to 13 percent. Growth described as "more slowly than the average" means an increase of 3 to 6 percent. "Little or no change" means a decrease of 2 percent to an increase of 2 percent. "Decline" means a decrease of 3 percent or more. Each article ends with **For More Information**, which lists organizations that provide information on training, education, internships, scholarships, and job placement.

Throughout the book you will also find illustrative photographs of some careers, informative sidebars, and interviews with professionals working in the design field. As you explore the wide variety of design careers that are presented in this book, consider which of them might best suit your personality, strengths, and general career goals. Be sure to contact the organizations listed at the end of each article for more information.

Architects

QUICK FACTS

School Subjects
Art
Mathematics

Personal Skills
Artistic
Communication/ideas

Work Environment
Primarily indoors
Primarily one location

Minimum Education Level
Bachelor's degree

Salary Range
$41,320 to $70,320 to
$119,220+

Certification or Licensing
Voluntary (certification)
Required (licensing)

Outlook
Faster than the average

DOT
001

GOE
02.07.03

NOC
2151

O*NET-SOC
17-1011.00

OVERVIEW

Architects plan, design, and observe construction of facilities used for human occupancy and of other structures. They consult with clients, plan layouts of buildings, prepare drawings of proposed buildings, write specifications, and prepare scale and full-sized drawings. Architects also may help clients to obtain bids, select a contractor, and negotiate the construction contract, and they also visit construction sites to ensure that the work is being completed according to specification. There are approximately 141,200 architects working in the United States.

HISTORY

Architecture began not with shelters for people to live in but with the building of religious structures—from Stonehenge in England and the pyramids in Egypt to pagodas in Japan and the Parthenon in Greece. It was the Romans who developed a new building method—concrete vaulting—that made possible large cities with permanent masonry buildings. As they extended the Roman Empire, they built for public and military purposes. They developed and built apartment buildings, law courts, public baths, theaters, and circuses. The industrial revolution with its demand for factories and mills developed iron and steel construction, which evolved into the steel and glass skyscraper of today.

Because the history of architecture follows that of human civilization, the architecture of any period reflects the culture of its people. Architecture of early periods has influenced that of later centuries, including the work of contemporary architects. The field continues

An architect explains the design process for the conversion of an office building to loft apartments to elected officials and businesspeople. (*Paul Efird, AP Photo*/Knoxville News-Sentinel)

to develop as new techniques and materials are discovered and as architects blend creativity with function.

THE JOB

The architect normally has two responsibilities: to design a building that will satisfy the client and to protect the public's health, safety, and welfare. This second responsibility requires architects to be licensed by the state in which they work. Meeting the first responsibility involves many steps. The job begins with learning what the client wants. The architect takes many factors into consideration, including local and state building and design regulations, climate, soil on which the building is to be constructed, zoning laws, fire regulations, and the client's financial limitations.

The architect then prepares a set of plans that, upon the client's approval, will be developed into final design and construction documents. These plans are typically created by using computer-aided design and drafting or building information modeling technology, although some architects still draw their designs by hand. The final design shows the exact dimensions of every portion of the building, including the location and size of columns and beams, electrical outlets and fixtures, plumbing, heating and air-conditioning facilities, windows, and doors. The architect works closely with consulting engineers on the specifics of the plumbing, heating, air-conditioning, and electrical work to be done.

The architect then assists the client in getting bids from general contractors, one of whom will be selected to construct the building to the specifications. The architect helps the client through the completion of the construction and occupancy phases, making certain the correct materials are used and that the drawings and specifications are faithfully followed.

Throughout the process the architect works closely with a design or project team. This team is usually made up of the following: *designers,* who specialize in design development; a *structural designer,* who designs the frame of the building in accordance with the work of the architect; the *project manager* or *job superintendent,* who sees that the full detail drawings are completed to the satisfaction of the architect; and the *specification writer* and *estimator,* who prepare a project manual that describes in more detail the materials to be used in the building, their quality and method of installation, and all details related to the construction of the building.

The architect's job is very complex. He or she is expected to know construction methods, engineering principles and practices, and materials. Architects also must be up to date on new design and construction techniques and procedures. Although architects once spent most of their time designing buildings for the wealthy, they are now more often involved in the design of housing developments, individual dwellings, supermarkets, industrial plants, office buildings, shopping centers, airport terminals, schools, banks, museums, churches, and structures of other religious faiths, and dozens of other types of buildings.

Architects may specialize in any one of a number of fields, including building appraisal, city planning, teaching, architectural journalism, furniture design, lighting design, or government service. Regardless of the area of specialization, the architect's major task is that of understanding the client's needs and then reconciling them into a meaningful whole.

REQUIREMENTS

High School

To prepare for this career while in high school, take a college preparatory program that includes courses in English, mathematics, physics, art (especially freehand drawing), social studies, history, and foreign languages. Courses in business and computer science also will be useful.

Postsecondary Training

Because most state architecture registration boards require a professional degree, high school students are advised, early in their senior year, to apply for admission to a professional program that is accredited by the National Architectural Accrediting Board. Competition to enter these programs is high. Grades, class rank, and aptitude and achievement scores count heavily in determining who will be accepted.

Most schools of architecture offer degrees through either a five-year bachelor's program or a three- or four-year master's program. The majority of architecture students seek out the bachelor's degree in architecture, going from high school directly into a five-year program. Though this is the fastest route, you should be certain that you want to study architecture. Because the programs are so specialized, it is difficult to transfer to another field of study if you change your mind. The master's degree option allows for more flexibility but takes longer to complete. In this case, students first earn a liberal arts degree then continue their training by completing a master's program in architecture. Visit http://www.acsa-arch.org/guide_search/home.aspx for a database of architecture schools in the United States and Canada.

A typical college architecture program includes courses in architectural history and theory, the technical and legal aspects of building design, science, and liberal arts.

Certification or Licensing

All states and the District of Columbia require that individuals be licensed before contracting to provide architectural services in that particular state. Though many work in the field without licensure, only licensed architects are required to take legal responsibility for all work. Using a licensed architect for a project is, therefore, less risky than using an unlicensed one. Architects who are licensed usually take on projects with larger responsibilities and have greater chances to advance to managerial or executive positions.

The requirements for registration include graduation from an accredited school of architecture and three years of practical experience (called an internship) with a licensed architect. After these requirements are met, individuals can take the rigorous Architect Registration Examination. Some states require architects to maintain their licensing through continued education. These individuals may complete a certain number of credits every year or two through seminars, workshops, university classes, self-study courses, or other sources.

In addition to becoming licensed, a growing number of architects choose to obtain certification by the National Council of Architectural Registration Boards. If an architect plans to work in more than one state, obtaining this certification can make it easier to become licensed in different states.

Other Requirements

If you are interested in architecture, you should be intelligent, observant, responsible, and self-disciplined. You should have a concern for detail and accuracy, be able to communicate effectively both orally and in writing, and be able to accept criticism constructively. Although great artistic ability is not necessary, you should be able to visualize spatial relationships and have the capacity to solve technical problems. Mathematical ability is also important. In addition, you should possess organizational skills and leadership qualities and be able to work well with others.

EXPLORING

Most architects will welcome the opportunity to talk with young people interested in entering architecture. You may be able to visit their offices to gain firsthand knowledge of the type of work done by architects. You can also visit a design studio of a school of architecture or work for an architect or building contractor during summer vacations. Also, many architecture schools offer summer programs for high school students. Books and magazines on architecture also can give you a broad understanding of the nature of the work and the values of the profession.

EMPLOYERS

Of the 141,200 architects working in the United States, approximately 68 percent are employed by architectural or engineering firms or other firms related to the construction industry. About 21 percent of architects, however, are self-employed—the ultimate dream of many people in the profession. A few develop graphic design, interior design, or product specialties. Still others put their training to work in the theater, film, or television fields, or in museums, display firms, and architectural product and materials manufacturing companies. A small number are employed in government agencies such as the Departments of Defense, Interior, and Housing and Urban Development and the General Services Administration.

STARTING OUT

Students entering architecture following graduation start as interns in an architectural firm. As interns, they assist in preparing architectural construction documents. They also handle related details, such as administering contracts, coordinating the work of other professionals on the project, researching building codes and construction materials, and writing specifications. As an alternative to working for an architectural firm, some architecture graduates go into allied fields such as construction, engineering, interior design, landscape architecture, or real estate development.

ADVANCEMENT

Interns and architects alike are given progressively more complex jobs. Architects may advance to supervisory or managerial positions. Some architects become partners in established firms, while others take steps to establish their own practice.

EARNINGS

Architects earned a median salary of $70,320 in 2008, according to the U.S. Department of Labor. The lowest paid 10 percent earned less than $41,320 annually, while the highest paid 10 percent earned $119,220 or more.

Well-established architects who are partners in an architectural firm or who have their own businesses generally earn much more than salaried employees. Most employers offer such fringe benefits as health insurance, sick and vacation pay, and retirement plans.

WORK ENVIRONMENT

Architects normally work a 40-hour week. There may be a number of times when they will have to work overtime, especially when under pressure to complete an assignment. Self-employed architects work less regular hours and often meet with clients in their homes or offices during the evening. Architects usually work in comfortable offices, but they may spend a considerable amount of time outside the office visiting clients or viewing the progress of a particular job in the field. Their routines usually vary considerably.

OUTLOOK

Employment in the field is expected to grow faster than the average for all occupations through 2018, according to the U.S. Department of Labor. The number of architects needed will depend on the volume of construction. The construction industry is extremely sensitive to fluctuations in the overall economy, and a bad economic climate could result in layoffs. In the next decade, employment is expected to be best in nonresidential construction. On the positive side, employment of architects is not likely to be affected by the growing use of computer technologies. Rather than replacing architects, computers are being used to enhance the architect's work.

Demographic trends will also play a strong role in fueling employment growth for architects. As a larger percentage of Americans reach the age of 65 and older, architects will be needed to design new healthcare facilities, nursing homes, and retirement communities. Aging educational facilities will also require the construction of new, larger, and more energy-efficient structures. Architects with knowledge of "green" or sustainable design techniques should have excellent employment opportunities.

Competition for employment will continue to be strong, particularly in prestigious architectural firms. Openings will not be newly created positions but will become available as the workload increases and established architects transfer to other occupations or leave the field.

FOR MORE INFORMATION

For information on education, jobs, scholarships, and student membership opportunities, contact
American Institute of Architects
1735 New York Avenue, NW
Washington, DC 20006-5292
Tel: 800-242-3837
E-mail: infocentral@aia.org
http://www.aia.org

For information on education, summer programs for high school students, and student membership opportunities, contact
American Institute of Architecture Students
1735 New York Avenue, NW
Washington, DC 20006-5292
Tel: 202-626-7472
E-mail: mailbox@aias.org
http://www.aiasnatl.org

For information on schools of architecture, contact
Association of Collegiate Schools of Architecture
1735 New York Avenue, NW
Washington, DC 20006-5292
Tel: 202-783-6500
http://www.acsa-arch.org

For information on certification, contact
National Council of Architectural Registration Boards
1801 K Street, NW, Suite 700-K
Washington, DC 20006-1301
Tel: 202-783-6500
http://www.ncarb.org

For information on careers in architecture, visit
ARCHcareers.org
http://www.archcareers.org

INTERVIEW

Tom Pope is a partner at Hartshorne Plunkard Architecture in Chicago, Illinois. He discussed his career with the editors of Careers in Focus: Design.

Q. Can you discuss Hartshorne Plunkard Architecture? What types of projects do you work on?

A. We are a team of 25 architects and designers, from various backgrounds, located in the Fulton Market District of Chicago. Our firm has been around for 20 years, started by Jim Plunkard and Ray Hartshorne. Our roots were in single-family homes and residential loft conversions, but over the past 15 years, our portfolio has included apartments, hotel, vacation and office, retail, institutional, entertainment, historical restoration, medical, financial work, and most recently, student housing. Our projects are mainly in the Chicagoland area, but we have done work in numerous other states over the years.

Q. What is one thing young people may not know about a career in architecture?

A. One thing you can never fully comprehend in design studio is the dynamic between the client, consultant, contractor, etc., until you actually get out into the real world of architecture. Once there, the learning curve goes up exponentially just by interacting with that group. You learn a lot more from your mistakes at this point than you will throughout the rest of your career.

Q. What do you like most and least about your job?

A. Most liked: I would say design, of course. However that means different things to different people. Most of our practical design is more so problem solving than high-design. It's the reality of architecture. So my most liked is the high-design, the point at which you can be the most creative. Least liked is an easy one, and it's inevitable in our business—claims. By far the least favorite part of the job is dealing with either claims made by the contractor as a result of drawing shortcomings, errors omissions, etc. It happens on *all* jobs, it comes down to how you handle these types of situations with the client that will make or break your relationship.

Q. What advice would you give to young people who are seeking to enter this career?

A. Stay positive and keep your mind open to whatever avenues are presented to you. There are many branches of architecture. You never know who you are going to meet that will later yield projects or other job opportunities. Your first job will be an eye-opener. You may not get to design things at first, but with persistence and hard work, you will find the profession very fulfilling.

Q. What is the employment outlook for architects?

A. With the economy at its current state, new jobs in this field are not available. What I mean by that is that the expansion of architects in the workforce now is currently more than the demand. But that doesn't mean that there are no opportunities. It means that the positions that ARE available will be filled by the most talented, prepared, and eloquent individuals who are willing to adapt to whatever is thrown at them. There are different levels of experience. There are those who have real experience—both technical and time-wise. And those who are just coming into the job market, with no experience, but have a certain level of maturity and confidence about their student work. Sometimes this level of confidence goes further than real experience, especially in dealing with people. People skills and technical/design ability are the most sought after. It's extremely competitive, now more so than it has been in the last five to 10 years. With the housing market imploding, clients/builders are seeking out new avenues of work and public-funded projects, school additions, infrastructure, rental, interior renovations, and student housing will be the market for the next five years and possibly beyond. Those who diversify their experience will do the best in this market.

Computer and Video Game Designers

OVERVIEW

Computer and video game designers create the ideas and interactivity for games. These games are played on various platforms, or media, such as video consoles and computers, on portable telecommunication devices (such as cell phones), and through online Internet subscriptions. They generate ideas for new game concepts, including sound effects, characters, story lines, and graphics. Designers either work for companies that make the games or create the games on their own and sell their ideas and programs to companies that produce them.

HISTORY

Computer and video game designers are a relatively new breed. The industry did not begin to develop until the 1960s and 1970s, when computer programmers at some large universities, big companies, and government labs began designing games on mainframe computers. Steve Russell was perhaps the first video game designer. In 1962, when he was in college, he made up a simple game called *Spacewar*. Graphics of space ships flew through a starry sky on the video screen, the object of the game being to shoot down enemy ships. Nolan Bushnell, another early designer, played *Spacewar* in college. In 1972 he put the first video game in an arcade; it was a game very much like *Spacewar,* and he called it *Computer Space*. However, many users found the game difficult to play, so it was not a success.

QUICK FACTS

School Subjects
Art
Computer science

Personal Skills
Communication/ideas
Technical/scientific

Work Environment
Primarily indoors
Primarily one location

Minimum Education Level
Bachelor's degree

Salary Range
$40,660 to $75,150 to
$114,830+

Certification or Licensing
None available

Outlook
Much faster than the average

DOT
N/A

GOE
01.04.02

NOC
2174

O*NET-SOC
15-1099.13

Bruce Artwick published the first of many versions of *Flight Simulator*, and Bushnell later created *Pong*, a game that required the players to paddle electronic ping-pong balls back and forth across the video screen. *Pong* was a big hit, and players spent thousands of quarters in arcade machines all over the country playing it. Bushnell's company, Atari, had to hire more and more designers every week, including Steve Jobs, Alan Kay, and Chris Crawford. These early designers made games with text-based descriptions (that is, no graphics) of scenes and actions with interactivity done through a computer keyboard. Games called *Adventure, Star Trek,* and *Flight Simulator* were among the first that designers created. They used simple commands like "look at building" and "move west." Most games were designed for video machines; not until the later 1970s did specially equipped TVs and early personal computers (PCs) begin appearing.

In the late 1970s and early 1980s, designers working for Atari and Intellivision made games for home video systems, PCs, and video arcades. Many of these new games had graphics, sound, text, and animation. Designers of games like *Pac-Man, Donkey Kong,* and *Space Invaders* were successful and popular. They also started to make role-playing games like the famous *Dungeons and Dragons*. Richard Garriott created *Ultima,* another major role-playing game. Games began to feature the names and photos of their programmers on the packaging, giving credit to individual designers.

Workers at Electronic Arts began to focus on making games for PCs to take advantage of technology that included the computer keyboard, more memory, and floppy disks. They created games like *Carmen Sandiego* and *M.U.L.E.* In the mid- to late 1980s, new technology included more compact floppies, sound cards, and larger memory. Designers also had to create games that would work on more than just one platform—PCs, Apple computers, and 64-bit video game machines.

In the 1990s, Electronic Arts started to hire teams of designers instead of "lone wolf" individuals (those who design games from start to finish independently). Larger teams were needed because games became more complex; design teams included not only programmers but also artists, musicians, writers, and animators. Designers made such breakthroughs as using more entertaining graphics, creating more depth in role-playing games, using virtual reality in sports games, and using more visual realism in racing games and flight simulators. This new breed of designers created games using techniques like Assembly, C, and HyperCard. By 1994, designers began to use CD-ROM technology to its fullest. In only a few months,

Doom was a hit. Designers of this game gave players the chance to alter it themselves at various levels, including choices of weapons and enemies. *Doom* still has fans worldwide.

The success of shareware (software that is given away to attract users to want to buy more complete software) has influenced the return of smaller groups of designers. Even the lone wolf is coming back, using shareware and better authoring tools such as sound libraries and complex multimedia development environments. Some designers are finding that they work best on their own or in small teams.

What is on the horizon for game designers? More multiplayer games; virtual reality; improved technology in coprocessors, chips, hardware, and sound fonts; and "persistent worlds," where online games are influenced by and evolve from players' actions. These new types of games require that designers know more and more complex code so that games can "react" to their multiple players.

THE JOB

Designing games involves programming code as well as creating stories, graphics, and sound effects. It is a very creative process, requiring imagination and computer and communication skills to develop games that are interactive and entertaining. As mentioned earlier, some game designers work on their own and try to sell their designs to companies that produce and distribute games; others are employees of companies such as Electronic Arts, Nintendo of America, and many others. Whether designers work alone or for a company, their aim is to create games that get players involved. Game players want to have fun, be challenged, and sometimes learn something along the way.

Each game must have a story line as well as graphics and sound that will entertain and engage the players. Story lines are situations that the players will find themselves in and make decisions about. Designers develop a plan for combining the story or concept, music or other sound effects, and graphics. They design rules to make it fun, challenging, or educational, and they create characters for the stories or circumstances, worlds in which these characters live, and problems or situations these characters will face.

One of the first steps is to identify the audience that will be playing the game. How old are the players? What kinds of things are they interested in? What kind of game will it be: action, adventure, "edutainment," role-playing, or sports? And which platform will the game use: video game system (e.g., Nintendo), wireless device (cell phone, PDA, etc.), computer (e.g., Macintosh), or online (Internet via subscription)?

The next steps are to create a design proposal, a preliminary design, and a final game design. The proposal is a brief summary of what the game involves. The preliminary design goes much further, outlining in more detail what the concept is (the story of the game); how the players get involved; what sound effects, graphics, and other elements will be included (What will the screen look like? What kinds of sound effects should the player hear?); and what productivity tools (such as word processors, database programs, spreadsheet programs, flow-charting programs, and prototyping programs) the designer intends to use to create these elements. Independent designers submit a product idea and design proposal to a publisher along with a cover letter and resume. Employees work as part of a team to create the proposal and design. Teamwork might include brainstorming sessions to come up with ideas, as well as involvement in market research (surveying the players who will be interested in the game).

The final game design details the basic idea, the plot, and every section of the game, including the startup process, all the scenes (such as innings for baseball games and maps for edutainment games), and all the universal elements (such as rules for scoring, names of characters, and a sound effect that occurs every time something specific happens). The story, characters, worlds, and maps are documented. The game design also includes details of the logic of the game, its algorithms (the step-by-step procedures for solving the problems the players will encounter), and its rules; the methods the player will use to load the game, start it up, score, win, lose, save, stop, and play again; the graphic design, including storyboards and sample art; and the audio design. The designer might also include marketing ideas and proposed follow-up games.

Designers interact with other workers and technologists involved in the game design project, including *programmers, audio engineers, artists,* and even *asset managers,* who coordinate the collecting, engineering, and distribution of physical assets to the *production team* (the people who will actually produce the physical CD-ROM or DVD).

Designers need to understand games and their various forms, think up new ideas, and experiment with and evaluate new designs. They assemble the separate elements (text, art, sound, video) of a game into a complete, interactive form, following through with careful planning and preparation (such as sketching out scripts, storyboards, and design documents). They write an implementation plan and guidelines (How will designers manage the process? How much will it cost to design the game? How long will the guidelines be—five

Did You Know?

- Sixty-eight percent of American households play computer or video games.
- Forty-two percent of U.S. households have a video game console.
- Forty percent of computer and video game players are female.
- The average game player is 35 years old. Twenty-five percent of gamers are over the age of 50.
- Thirty-seven percent of Americans play games on wireless devices such as cell phones or PDAs.
- In 2008, computer and video game sales reached a record $11.7 billion.
- The most popular computer game genres (by units sold) in 2008 were strategy (34.6 percent), role-playing (19.6 percent), family entertainment (17.1 percent), shooter (9.7 percent), adventure (6.8 percent), children's entertainment (2.5 percent), action (2.7 percent), sports (1.8 percent), flight (1.8 percent), other games/compilations (1.4 percent), racing (1.4 percent), and arcade (0.5 percent).

Source: *Essential Facts About the Computer and Video Game Industry, 2009*

pages? 300?). Finally, they amend designs at every stage, solving problems and answering questions.

Computer and video game designers often keep scrapbooks, notes, and journals of interesting ideas and other bits of information. They collect potential game material and even catalog ideas, videos, movies, pictures, stories, character descriptions, music clips, sound effects, animation sequences, and interface techniques. The average time it takes to design a game, including all the elements and stages just described, can be from about six to 18 months.

REQUIREMENTS

High School

If you like to play video or computer games, you are already familiar with them. You will also need to learn a programming language like C++ or Java, and you'll need a good working knowledge of the hardware platform for which you plan to develop your games (video, computer, online, etc.). In high school, learn as much as you can about computers: how they work, what kinds there are, how to program them, and any languages you can learn. You should also take physics, chemistry, and computer science. Since designers are creative, take courses such as art, literature, and music as well.

Postsecondary Training

Although strictly speaking you don't have to have a college degree to be a game designer, most companies are looking for creative people who also have a degree. Having one represents that you've been actively involved in intense, creative work; that you can work with others and follow through on assignments; and, of course, that you've learned what there is to know about programming, computer architecture (including input devices, processing devices, memory and storage devices, and output devices), and software engineering. Employers want to know that you've had some practical experience in design.

A growing number of schools offer courses or degrees in game design. Animation World Network offers a database of animation schools at its Web site, http://schools.awn.com. Another good source of schools can be found at the International Game Developers Association's Web site, http://www.igda.org/breakingin/resource_schools.php.

Recommended college courses include programming (including assembly level), computer architecture, software engineering, computer graphics, data structures, algorithms, game design, communication networks, artificial intelligence (AI) and expert systems, interface systems, mathematics, and physics.

Other Requirements

One major requirement for game design is that you must love to play computer games. You need to continually keep up with technology, which changes fast. Although you might not always use them, you need to have a variety of skills, such as writing stories, programming, and designing sound effects.

You must also have vision and the ability to identify your players and anticipate their every move in your game. You'll also have to be able to communicate well with programmers, writers, artists, musicians, electronics engineers, production workers, and others.

You must have the endurance to see a project through from beginning to end and also be able to recognize when a design should be scrapped.

EXPLORING

One of the best ways to learn about game design is to try to develop copies of easy games, such as *Pong* and *Pac-Man,* or try to change a game that has an editor. (Games like *Klik & Play, Empire,* and *Doom* allow players to modify them to create new circumstances and settings.)

For high school students interested in finding out more about how video games and animations are produced, the DigiPen Institute of Technology (https://workshops.digipen.edu/workshops/overview) offers summer workshops. Two-week courses are offered throughout the summer, providing hands-on experience and advice on courses to take in high school to prepare yourself for postsecondary training.

Writing your own stories, puzzles, and games helps develop storytelling and problem-solving skills. Magazines such as *Computer Graphics World* (http://www.cgw.com) and *Game Developer* (http://www.gdmag.com) have articles about digital video and high-end imaging and other technical and design information.

EMPLOYERS

Software publishers (such as Electronic Arts and Activision Blizzard) are found throughout the country, though most are located in California, New York, Washington State, and Illinois. Big media companies such as Disney have also opened interactive entertainment departments. Jobs should be available at these companies as well as with online services and interactive networks, which are growing rapidly. Visit http://aidb.com for a database of thousands of animation-related companies.

Some companies are involved in producing games only for wireless devices or online play; others produce only for computers; others make games for various platforms.

STARTING OUT

There are a couple of ways to begin earning money as a game designer: independently or as an employee of a company. It is more realistic to get any creative job you can in the industry (for example, as an artist, a play tester, a programmer, or a writer) and learn as you go, developing your design skills as you work your way up to the level of designer.

Contact company Web sites and sites that advertise job openings, such as Animation World Network (http://www.awn.com), Highend Careers (http://www.highendcareers.com), GameJobs.com (http://www.gamejobs.com), Gamasutra (http://www.gamasutra.com), and Dice (http://www.dice.com).

In addition to a professional resume, it is a good idea to have your own Web site, where you can showcase your demos. Make sure you have designed at least one demo or have an impressive portfolio of design ideas and documents.

Other ways to find a job in the industry include going to job fairs (such as the Game Developers Conference, http://www.gdconf.com), where you find recruiters looking for creative people to work at their companies, and checking in with online user groups, which often post jobs on the Internet.

Also consider looking for an internship to prepare for this career. Many software and entertainment companies hire interns for short-term assignments.

ADVANCEMENT

Just as with many jobs, to have better opportunities to advance their position and possibly earn more money, computer and video game designers have to keep up with technology. They must be willing to constantly learn more about design, the industry, and even financial and legal matters involved in development.

Becoming and remaining great at their job may be a career-long endeavor for computer and video game designers, or just a stepping-stone to another area of interactive entertainment. Some designers start out as artists, writers, or programmers, learning enough in these jobs to eventually design. For example, a person entering this career may begin as a 3-D animation modeler and work on enough game life cycles to understand what it takes to be a game designer. He or she may decide to specialize in another area, such as sound effects or even budgeting.

Some designers rise to management positions, such as president or vice president of a software publisher. Others write for magazines and books, teach, or establish their own game companies.

EARNINGS

Most development companies spend up to two years designing a game even before any of the mechanics (such as writing final code and drawing final graphics) begin; more complex games take even longer. Companies budget $1 million to $3 million for developing just one game. If the game is a success, designers are often rewarded with bonuses. In addition to bonuses or royalties (the percentage of profits designers receive from each game that is sold), designers' salaries are affected by their amount of professional experience, their location in the country, and the size of their employer.

Game Developer magazine reports that game designers had average salaries of approximately $67,379 in 2008. Game designers with less than three years of experience earned approximately $46,208. Those with three to six years' experience averaged $54,716 annually, and those with more than six years' experience averaged $74,688 per year. Lead designers/creative directors earned higher salaries, ranging from $60,833 for those with three to six years' experience to $98,370 for workers with six or more years of experience in the field. It is important to note that these salaries are averages, and some designers (especially those at the beginning stages of their careers) earn less than these amounts. These figures, however, provide a useful guide for the range of earnings available. Game designers on the West Coast earn salaries that are approximately 12 percent higher than those employed in other parts of the company, according to *Game Developer*.

The U.S Department of Labor reports that in 2008 video game developers earned salaries that ranged from less than $40,660 to more than $114,803, with median earnings of $75,150.

Any major software publisher will likely provide benefits such as medical insurance, paid vacations, and retirement plans. Designers who are self-employed must provide their own benefits.

WORK ENVIRONMENT

Computer and video game designers work in office settings, whether at a large company or a home studio. At some companies, artists and designers sometimes find themselves working 24 or 48 hours at a time, so the office areas are set up with sleeping couches and other areas where employees can relax. Because the game development industry is competitive, many designers find themselves under a lot of pressure from deadlines, design problems, and budget concerns.

OUTLOOK

Computer and video games are a fast-growing segment of the U.S. entertainment industry. In fact, the Entertainment Software Association reports that sales of computer and video game software reached $9.5 billion in 2007. As the demand for new games, more sophisticated games, and games to be played on new systems grows, more and more companies will hire skilled people to create and perfect these products. Opportunities for game designers, therefore, should be good.

In any case, game development is popular; the Entertainment Software Association estimates that about 36 percent of American heads of households play computer and video games. People in the industry expect more and more integration of interactive entertainment into mainstream society. Online development tools such as engines, graphic and sound libraries, and programming languages such as Java will probably create opportunities for new types of products that can feature game components.

FOR MORE INFORMATION

For industry information, contact
   Academy of Interactive Arts and Sciences
   23622 Calabasas Road, Suite 220
   Calabasas, CA 91302-4111
   Tel: 818-876-0826
   http://www.interactive.org

For industry information, contact
   Entertainment Software Association
   575 7th Street, NW, Suite 300
   Washington, DC 20004-1611
   E-mail: esa@theesa.com
   http://www.theesa.com

For comprehensive career information, including Breaking In: Preparing For Your Career in Games, *visit the IGDA Web site.*
   International Game Developers Association (IGDA)
   19 Mantua Road
   Mt. Royal, NJ 08061-1006
   Tel: 856-423-2990
   http://www.igda.org

Costume Designers

OVERVIEW

Costume designers plan, create, and maintain clothing and accessories for all characters in stage, film, television, dance, or opera productions. Designers custom fit each character, and either create a new garment or alter an existing costume.

HISTORY

Costume design has been an important part of the theater since the early Greek tragedies, when actors generally wore masks and long robes with sleeves. By the time of the Roman Caesars, stage costumes had become very elaborate and colorful.

After the fall of Rome, theater disappeared for some time, but later returned in the form of Easter and Nativity plays. Priests and choirboys wore their usual robes with some simple additions, such as veils and crowns. Plays then moved from the church to the marketplace, and costumes again became important to the production.

During the Renaissance, costumes were designed for the Italian pageants, the French ballets, and the English masques by such famous designers as Torelli, Jean Berain, and Lodovico Ottavio Burnacini. From 1760 to 1782, Louis-Rene Boquet designed costumes using wide paniers, forming a kind of elaborate ballet skirt. But by the end of the 18th century, there was a movement toward more classical costumes on the stage.

During the early 19th century, historical costumes became popular, and period details were added to contemporary dress. Toward the end of the 19th century, realism became important, and actors wore the dress of the day, often their own clothes. Because this trend resulted in less work for the costume designers, they turned to musical and opera productions to express their creativity.

In the early 20th century, Sergei Pavlovich Diaghilev's Russian Ballet introduced a nonnaturalism in costumes, most notably in the designs of Leon Bakst. This trend gave way to European avant-garde theater, in which costumes became abstract and symbolic.

Since the 1960s, new materials, such as plastics and adhesives, have greatly increased the costume designer's range. Today, their work is prominent in plays, musicals, dance performances, films, music videos, and television programs.

THE JOB

Costume designers generally work as freelancers. After they have been contracted to provide the costumes for a production, they read the script to learn about the theme, location, time period, character types, dialogue, and action. They meet with the director to discuss his or her feelings on the plot, characters, period and style, time frame for the production, and budget.

For a play, designers plan a rough costume plot, which is a list of costume changes by scene for each character. They thoroughly research the history and setting in which the play is set. They plan a preliminary color scheme and sketch the costumes, including details such as gloves, footwear, hose, purses, jewelry, canes, fans, bouquets, and other props. The costume designer or an assistant collects swatches of fabrics and samples of various accessories.

After completing the research, final color sketches are painted or drawn and mounted for presentation. Once the director approves the designs, the costume designer solicits bids from contractors, creates or rents costumes, and shops for fabrics and accessories. Measurements of all actors are taken. Designers work closely with drapers, sewers, hairstylists, and makeup artists in the costume shop. They supervise fittings and attend all dress rehearsals to make final adjustments and repairs.

Costume designers also create costumes for films, television, and videos, aiming to provide the look that will highlight characters' personalities. Aside from working with actors, they may also design and create costumes for performers such as figure skaters, ballroom dance competitors, circus members, theme park characters, rock artists, and others who routinely wear costumes as part of a show.

Award-Winning Designs

Costume designers are an important part of any motion picture production. The following is a list of costume designers and films that have won the Academy Award for Costume Design. Watch some of these films and consider how the costumes reflect the characters, time period, and overall style of the film.

2009: Sandy Powell, *The Young Victoria*

2008: Michael O'Connor, *The Duchess*

2007: Alexandra Byrne, *Elizabeth: The Golden Age*

2006: Milena Canonero, *Marie Antoinette*

2005: Colleen Atwood, *Memoirs of a Geisha*

2004: Sandy Powell, *The Aviator*

2003: Ngila Dickinson and Richard Taylor, *The Lord of the Rings: The Return of the King*

2002: Colleen Atwood, *Chicago*

2001: Catherine Martin and Angus Strathie, *Moulin Rouge*

2000: Janty Yates, *Gladiator*

1999: Lindy Hemming, *Topsy-Turvy*

1998: Sandy Powell, *Shakespeare in Love*

1997: Deborah L. Scott, *Titanic*

1996: Ann Roth, *The English Patient*

1995: James Acheson, *Restoration*

Source: Academy of Motion Picture Arts and Sciences, http://www.oscar.org

REQUIREMENTS

High School

Costume designers need at least a high school education. It is helpful to take classes in art, home economics, and theater and to participate in drama clubs or community theater. English, literature, and history classes will help you learn how to analyze a play and research the clothing and manner of various historical periods. Marketing and business-related classes will also be helpful, as most costume designers work as freelancers. Familiarity with computers is useful, as many designers work with computer-aided design and drafting (CADD) programs.

While in high school, consider starting a portfolio of design sketches. Practicing in a sketchbook is a great way to get ideas and designs out on paper and organized for future reference. You can also get design ideas through others; watch theater, television, or movie productions and take note of the characters' dress. Sketch them on your own for practice. Looking through fashion magazines can also give you ideas to sketch.

Postsecondary Training

A college degree is not a requirement, but in this highly competitive field, it gives a sizable advantage. Most costume designers today have a bachelor's degree. Many art schools, especially in New York and Los Angeles, have programs in costume design at both the bachelor's and master's degree level. A liberal arts school with a strong theater program is also a good choice.

Other Requirements

Costume designers need sewing, draping, and patterning skills, as well as training in basic design techniques and figure drawing. Aside from being artistic, designers must have good people skills because many compromises and agreements must be made between the designer and the production's director.

Costume designers must prepare a portfolio of their work, including photographs and sketches highlighting their best efforts. Some theatrical organizations require membership in United Scenic Artists (USA), a union that protects the interests of designers on the job and sets minimum fees. Students in design programs who pass an exam and have some design experience can apply for USA's Designer Apprentice Program. More experienced designers who want full professional membership in the union must also submit a portfolio for review.

EXPLORING

If you are interested in costume design, consider joining a theater organization, such as a school drama club or a community theater. School dance troupes or film classes also may offer opportunities to explore costume design.

The Costume Designer's Handbook: A Complete Guide for Amateur and Professional Costume Designers, by Rosemary Ingham and Liz Covey (Portsmouth, N.H.: Heinemann Drama, 1992), is an invaluable resource for beginning or experienced costume designers. Another useful title is *Costume Design 101: The Business and Art of Creating Costumes for Film and Television,* 2d ed., by Richard La Motte (Studio City, Calif.: Michael Wiese Productions, 2010).

You can practice designing on your own, by drawing original sketches or copying designs from television, films, or the stage. Practice sewing and altering costumes from sketches for yourself, friends and family.

EMPLOYERS

Costume designers are employed by production companies that produce works for stage, television, and film. Most employers are located in New York and Los Angeles, although most metropolitan areas have community theater and film production companies that hire designers.

STARTING OUT

Most high schools and colleges have drama clubs and dance groups that need costumes designed and made. Community theaters, too, may offer opportunities to assist in costume production. Regional theaters hire several hundred costume technicians each year for seasons that vary from 28 to 50 weeks.

Many beginning designers enter the field by becoming an assistant to a designer. Many established designers welcome newcomers and can be generous mentors. Some beginning workers start out in costume shops, which usually requires membership in a union. However, nonunion workers may be allowed to work for short-term projects. Some designers begin as *shoppers,* who swatch fabrics, compare prices, and buy yardage, trim, and accessories. Shoppers learn where to find the best materials at reasonable prices and often establish valuable contacts in the field. Other starting positions include milliner's assistant, craft assistant, or assistant to the draper.

Schools with bachelor's and master's programs in costume design may offer internships that can lead to jobs after graduation. Another method of entering costume design is to contact regional theaters directly and send your resume to the theater's managing director.

Before you become a costume designer, you may want to work as a freelance design assistant for a few years to gain helpful experience, a reputation, contacts, and an impressive portfolio.

ADVANCEMENT

Beginning designers must show they are willing to do a variety of tasks. The theater community is small and intricately interconnected, so those who work hard and are flexible with assignments can gain good reputations quickly. Smaller regional theaters tend to hire designers for a full season to work with the same people on one or more productions, so opportunities for movement may be scarce. Eventually, costume designers with experience and talent can work for larger productions, such as films, television, and videos.

EARNINGS

Earnings vary greatly in this business depending on factors such as how many outfits the designer completes, how long they are employed during the year, and the amount of their experience. Although the U.S. Department of Labor does not provide salary figures for costume designers, it does report that the related occupational group of fashion designers had a median hourly wage of $29.41 in 2008. For full-time work, this hourly wage translates into a yearly income of approximately $61,160. However, those just starting out and working as assistants earned as little as $15.46 an hour, translating into an annual salary of approximately $32,150. The most experienced fashion designers earned $59.99 and hour, or $124,780 annually.

Costume designers who work on Broadway or for other large stage productions are usually members of the United Scenic Artists union, which sets minimum fees, requires producers to pay into pension and welfare funds, protects the designer's rights, establishes rules for billing, and offers group health and life insurance.

According to the union, a costume designer for a Broadway show (dramatic) in 2009 earned anywhere from $7,332 (for creating costumes for shows with one to seven characters) to $16,463 (for shows with 36 or more characters). For opera and dance companies, salary is usually by costume count. Costume designers working on major film or television productions earned union minimums of $2,776 for five days of work in 2009.

For feature films and television, costume designers earn daily rates for an eight-hour day or a weekly rate for an unlimited number of hours. Designers sometimes earn royalties on their designs. The U.S. Department of Labor reports that mean annual earnings for salaried fashion designers working in the motion picture and video industries were $89,760 in 2008.

Regional theaters usually set individual standard fees, which vary widely, beginning around $200 per week for an assistant. Most of them do not require membership in the union.

Most costume designers work freelance and are paid per costume or show. Costume designers can charge $90 to $500 per costume, but some costumes, such as those for figure skaters, can cost thousands of dollars. Freelance costume designers often receive a flat rate for designing costumes for a show. For small and regional theaters, this rate may be in the $400 to $500 range; the flat rate for medium and large productions generally starts at around $1,000. Many costume designers must take second part-time or full-time jobs to supplement their income from costume design.

Freelancers are responsible for their own health insurance, life insurance, and pension plans. They do not receive holiday, sick, or vacation pay.

WORK ENVIRONMENT

Costume designers put in long hours at painstaking detail work. It is a demanding profession that requires flexible, artistic, and practical workers. The schedule can be erratic—a busy period followed by weeks of little or no work. Though costumes are often a crucial part of a production's success, designers usually get little recognition compared to the actors and director.

Designers meet a variety of interesting and gifted people. Every play, film, or concert is different and every production situation is unique, so there is rarely a steady routine. Costume designers must play many roles: artist, sewer, researcher, buyer, manager, and negotiator.

OUTLOOK

The U.S. Department of Labor predicts that employment for fashion designers (a category that includes costume designers) will experience little or no growth compared to all careers through 2018. The health of the entertainment business, especially theater, is very dependent on the overall economy and public attitudes. Theater budgets and government support for the arts in general have come under pressure in recent years and have limited employment prospects for costume designers. Many theaters, especially small and nonprofit theaters, are cutting their budgets or doing smaller shows that require fewer costumes. Additionally, people are less willing to spend money on tickets or go to theaters during economic downturns or times of crisis.

Nevertheless, opportunities for costume designers exist. As more cable television networks create original programming, demand for costume design in this area is likely to increase. Costume designers are able to work in an increasing number of locations as new regional theaters and cable television companies operate throughout the United States. As a result, however, designers must be willing to travel.

Competition for designer jobs is stiff and will remain so throughout the next decade. The number of qualified costume designers far exceeds the number of jobs available. This is especially true in smaller cities and regions, where there are fewer theaters.

FOR MORE INFORMATION

This union represents costume designers in film and television. For information on the industry and to view costume sketches in their online gallery, contact the guild or check out its Web site.

Costume Designers Guild
11969 Ventura Boulevard, 1st Floor
Studio City, CA 91604-2630
Tel: 818-752-2400
E-mail: cdgia@costumedesignersguild.com
http://www.costumedesignersguild.com

For information on costume design, contact
Costume Society of America
390 Amwell Road, Suite 402
Hillsborough, NJ 08844-1247
Tel: 800-272-9447
E-mail: national.office@costumesocietyamerica.com
http://www.costumesocietyamerica.com

For information on scholarships, contact
National Costumers Association
121 North Bosart Avenue
Indianapolis, IN 46201-3729
Tel: 317-351-1940
E-mail: office@costumers.org
http://www.costumers.org

This union represents costume designers and other design professionals. For information on membership, apprenticeship programs, and other resources on the career, contact
United Scenic Artists Local USA 829
29 West 38th Street
New York, NY 10018-5504
Tel: 212-581-0300
http://www.usa829.org

For additional information, contact
United States Institute for Theater Technology
315 South Crouse Avenue, Suite 200
Syracuse, NY 13210-1844
Tel: 800-938-7488
http://www.usitt.org

Drafters

OVERVIEW

Drafters prepare working plans and detailed drawings of products or structures from the rough sketches, specifications, and calculations of engineers, architects, and designers. These drawings are used in engineering or manufacturing processes to reproduce exactly the product or structure desired, according to the specified dimensions. The drafter uses knowledge of various machines, engineering practices, mathematics, and building materials, along with other physical sciences and fairly extensive computer skills, to complete the drawings. There are approximately 251,900 drafters working in the United States.

HISTORY

In industry, drafting is the conversion of ideas from people's minds to precise working specifications from which products can be made. Many people find it much easier to give visual rather than oral or written directions, and to assemble new equipment if the instructions include diagrams and drawings. Often, this is especially true in complex situations or when a large number of people are involved; drawings allow all aspects to be addressed and everyone to receive the same information at the same time. Industry has come to rely on drafters to develop the working specifications from the new ideas and findings of people in laboratories, shops, factories, and design studios.

Until the 1970s, drafting and designing were done with a pencil and paper on a drafting table. While some drafters still use pencil

QUICK FACTS

School Subjects
Art
Computer science
Mathematics

Personal Skills
Artistic
Technical/scientific

Work Environment
Primarily indoors
Primarily one location

Minimum Education Level
Some postsecondary training

Salary Range
$28,220 to $44,490 to $79,790+

Certification or Licensing
Recommended (certification)
Required for certain positions (licensing)

Outlook
More slowly than the average

DOT
017

GOE
02.08.03

NOC
2253

O*NET-SOC
17-3011.00, 17-3011.01, 17-3011.02, 17-3012.00, 17-3012.01, 17-3012.02, 17-3013.00

and paper to create drawings, most use computer-assisted design and drafting (CADD) technology. Today, there are tens of thousands of CADD workstations in industrial settings. CADD systems greatly speed up and simplify the designer's and drafter's work. They do more than just let the operator "draw" the technical illustration on the screen. They add the speed and power of computer processing, plus software with technical information that ease the designer/drafter's tasks. CADD systems make complex mathematical calculations, spot problems, offer advice, and provide a wide range of other assistance. Today, nearly all drafting tasks are done with such equipment.

As the Internet has developed, CADD operators can send a CADD drawing across the world in a matter of minutes attached to an e-mail message. Gone are the days of rolling up a print and mailing it off via snail mail. Technology has once again made work more efficient for the CADD designer and drafter.

THE JOB

The drafter prepares detailed plans and specification drawings from the ideas, notes, or rough sketches of scientists, engineers, architects, and designers. Sometimes drawings are developed after a visit to a project in the field or as the result of a discussion with one or more people involved in the job. The drawings, which usually provide a number of different views of the object, must be exact and accurate. Such drawings usually include information concerning the quality of materials to be used, their cost, and the processes to be followed in carrying out the job. In developing drawings made to scale of the object to be built, most drafters use CADD systems. Technicians work at specially designed and equipped interactive computer graphics workstations. They call up computer files that hold data about a new product; they then run the programs to convert that information into diagrams and drawings of the product. These are displayed on a video display screen, which then acts as an electronic drawing board. Following the directions of an engineer or designer, the drafter enters changes to the product's design into the computer. The drafter merges these changes into the data file, and then displays the corrected diagrams and drawings.

The software in CADD systems is very helpful to the user—it offers suggestions and advice and even points out errors. The most important advantage of working with a CADD system is that it saves the drafter from the lengthy process of having to produce, by hand, the original and then the revised product drawings and diagrams.

The CADD workstation is equipped to allow drafters to perform calculations, develop simulations, and manipulate and modify the displayed material. Using typed commands at a keyboard, a stylus or light pen for touching the screen display, a mouse, joystick, or other electronic methods of interacting with the display, drafters can move, rotate, or zoom in on any aspect of the drawing on the screen, and project 3-D images from 2-D sketches. They can make experimental changes to the design and then run tests on the modified design to determine its qualities, such as weight, strength, flexibility, and the cost of materials that would be required. Compared to traditional drafting and design techniques, CADD offers virtually unlimited freedom to explore alternatives, and in far less time.

When the product design is completed and the necessary information is assembled in the computer files, drafters may store the newly developed data, output it on a printer, transfer it to another computer, or send it directly to another step of the automated testing or manufacturing process.

Drafters often are classified according to the type of work they do or their level of responsibility. Senior drafters use the preliminary information and ideas provided by engineers and architects to make design layouts. They may have the title of *chief drafter,* and so assign work to other drafters and supervise their activities. *Detailers* make complete drawings, giving dimensions, material, and any other necessary information of each part shown on the layout. *Checkers* carefully examine drawings to check for errors in computing or in recording dimensions and specifications.

Drafters also may specialize in a particular field of work, such as mechanical, electrical, electronic, aeronautical, structural, civil, or architectural drafting. Although the nature of the work of drafters is not too different from one specialization to another, there is a considerable variation in the type of object with which they deal. The following paragraphs detail specialties in the construction industry and other fields.

Commercial drafters do all-around drafting, such as plans for building sites, layouts of offices and factories, and drawings of charts, forms, and records.

Civil drafters make construction drawings for roads and highways, river and harbor improvements, flood control, drainage, and other civil engineering projects. *Structural drafters* draw plans for bridge trusses, plate girders, roof trusses, trestle bridges, and other structures that use structural reinforcing steel, concrete, masonry, and other structural materials.

Cartographic drafters prepare maps of geographic areas to show natural and constructed features, political boundaries, and other features. *Topographical drafters* draft and correct maps from original sources, such as other maps, surveying notes, and aerial photographs. *Architectural drafters* draw plans of buildings, including artistic and structural features. *Landscape drafters* make detailed drawings from sketches furnished by landscape architects.

Heating and ventilating drafters draft plans for heating, air-conditioning, ventilating, and sometimes refrigeration equipment. *Plumbing drafters* draw diagrams for the installation of plumbing equipment. *Mechanical drafters* make working drawings of machinery, automobiles, power plants, or any mechanical device. *Castings drafters* prepare detailed drawings of castings, which are objects formed in a mold. *Tool design drafters* draft manufacturing plans for all kinds of tools. *Patent drafters* make drawings of mechanical devices for use by lawyers to obtain patent rights for their clients.

Electrical drafters make schematics and wiring diagrams to be used by construction crews working on equipment and wiring in power plants, communications centers, buildings, or electrical distribution systems. *Electronics drafters* draw schematics and wiring diagrams for television cameras and TV sets, radio transmitters and receivers, computers, radiation detectors, and other electronic equipment.

Electromechanisms design drafters draft designs of electromechanical equipment such as aircraft engines, data processing systems, gyroscopes, automatic materials handling and processing machinery, or biomedical equipment. *Electromechanical drafters* draw wiring diagrams, layouts, and mechanical details for the electrical components and systems of a mechanical process or device.

Aeronautical drafters prepare engineering drawings for planes, missiles, and spacecraft. *Automotive design drafters* and *automotive design layout drafters* both turn out working layouts and master drawings of components, assemblies, and systems of automobiles and other vehicles. Automotive design drafters make original designs from specifications, and automotive design layout drafters make drawings based on prior layouts or sketches. *Marine drafters* draft the structural and mechanical features of ships, docks, and marine buildings and equipment. Projects range from petroleum drilling platforms to nuclear submarines.

Geological drafters make diagrams and maps of geological formations and locations of mineral, oil, and gas deposits. *Geophysical drafters* draw maps and diagrams based on data from petroleum prospecting instruments such as seismographs, gravity meters, and magnetometers. *Directional survey drafters* plot bore holes for oil and gas wells. *Process piping* or *pipeline drafters* draft plans for the construction and operation of oil fields, refineries, and pipeline systems.

A design team working on electrical or gas power plants and substations may be headed by a *chief design drafter,* who oversees architectural, electrical, mechanical, and structural drafters. *Estimators* and drafters draw specifications and instructions for installing voltage transformers, cables, and other electrical equipment that delivers electric power to consumers.

REQUIREMENTS

High School

If you are interested in a career as a drafter, begin your preparation in high school. Be sure to take many mathematics classes—especially algebra, geometry, and trigonometry. If your school offers courses in mechanical drawing, take as many as you can. If mechanical drawing is not available, take some art classes. Wood, metal, or electric shop may be helpful, depending on the field specialty in which you're interested. Geography or earth science courses are also useful. Finally, enroll in any computer classes you can, especially those in computer-aided design; increased familiarity with technology will strengthen your job prospects.

Postsecondary Training

Preparation beyond high school (including courses in the physical sciences, mathematics, drawing, sketching and drafting techniques, and in other technical areas) is essential for certain types of beginning positions, as well as for advancement to positions of greater salary and more responsibility. This training is available through technical institutes, community colleges, and four-year universities. However, the quality of programs varies greatly, so you should be careful about choosing one that meets your needs. Ask potential employers about their educational preferences, and check the qualifications of various schools' faculties. Generally, two-year community college programs that lead to an associate's degree offer a more well-rounded education than those provided by technical schools. Also, four-year colleges typically do not offer specific drafting training but have courses in areas such as engineering and architecture.

With respect to choosing a school for advanced training in drafting, exposure to CADD technology has become a necessity. Keep in mind, however, that CADD is a tool; it can help if manual drawing skill is not your strong suit: It does not replace knowledge and experience, or creativity and imagination. A thorough grounding in the traditional drawing methods of drafting is as vitally important today as facility with CADD.

Certification or Licensing

Certification is not presently required but is recommended in this field. More and more, employers are looking for graduates whose skills have been approved by a reliable industry source. The American Design Drafting Association/American Digital Design Association (ADDA) offers certification; becoming certified not only will enhance your credibility as a professional but could give you an edge in the job market.

ADDA also certifies schools that offer a drafting curriculum. As with individual certification, this accreditation process is not yet mandatory (although it can be a help to applicants in choosing where they'd like to receive training). Increasingly, however, states have begun to require that schools be ADDA-accredited (in order to receive grant funding, for instance). This suggests that required certification, and perhaps licensing, may be on the horizon.

Licensing requirements vary. Licensing may be required for specific projects, such as a construction project, when the client requires it.

Other Requirements

Students interested in drafting should have a good sense of both spatial perception (the ability to visualize objects in two or three dimensions) and formal perception (the ability to compare and discriminate between shapes, lines, forms, and shadings). Good hand-eye coordination is also necessary for the fine detail work involved in drafting.

EXPLORING

High school programs provide several opportunities for gaining experience in drafting. Mechanical drawing and computer-aided design are good courses to take. There are also many hobbies and leisure activities, such as woodworking, building models, and repairing and remodeling projects, that require the preparation of drawings or use of blueprints. After the completion of some courses in mechanical drawing or computer-aided design, it may be possible to locate a part-time or summer job in drafting.

EMPLOYERS

Approximately 251,900 drafters are employed in the United States, with approximately 52 percent employed by architectural, engineering, and related services firms that design construction projects. Others work in manufacturing, in automotive or aerospace design, for heavy equipment manufacturers—almost anywhere where the end product must meet precise specifications. Other drafters work for transportation, communications, or utilities companies, or for local, state, or federal agencies. If a student has a particular interest in almost any field plus a desire to become a drafter, chances are good that he or she can find a job that will combine the two. Architectural and civil drafters account for 47 percent of all drafters; 31 percent are mechanical drafters, and 13 percent are electrical and electronics drafters.

STARTING OUT

Beginning drafters generally have graduated from a postsecondary program at a technical institute or junior college. Skill certification through the American Design Drafting Association/American Digital Design Association may be advantageous. Applicants for government positions may need to take a civil service examination. Students with some formal postsecondary technical training often qualify for positions as *junior drafters* who revise detail drawings and then gradually assume drawing assignments of a more complex nature.

ADVANCEMENT

With additional experience and skill, beginning drafters become checkers, detailers, design drafters, or senior drafters. Movement from one to another of these job classifications is not restricted; each business modifies work assignments based on its own needs. Drafters often move into related positions. Some typical positions include technical report writers, sales engineers, engineering assistants, production foremen, and installation technicians.

EARNINGS

Earnings in this field are dependent on a number of factors including skills and experience. Students with more extensive advanced training tend to earn higher beginning salaries. Salaries also are affected by regional demands in specific specialties, so where a drafter chooses to live and work will play a part in his or her salary.

According to the U.S. Department of Labor, median annual earnings of architectural and civil drafters were $44,490 in 2008. Earnings ranged from less than $28,220 for the lowest paid 10 percent to more than $67,110 for the highest paid 10 percent. Median annual earnings of mechanical drafters were $46,640 in 2008, with a range of less than $29,390 for the lowest paid 10 percent to more than

$71,340 for the highest paid 10 percent. Median earnings of electrical and electronics drafters were $51,320 a year in 2008. The lowest paid 10 percent of electrical and electronics drafters earned less than $32,050 a year, and the highest paid 10 percent earned more than $79,790. According to Salary.com, CADD drafters earned salaries that ranged from less than $36,034 to $57,154 or more in 2009.

Employers generally offer drafters a range of benefit options, including health insurance, retirement plans, and the like. Travel sometimes is considered an indirect benefit of a job. Although architects and engineers often travel to construction sites to inspect the development of individual projects, drafters seldom are required to travel. Construction drafters, for instance, may be asked to visit sites toward the end of construction to provide final drawings of the completed structure, but most of their work will be done from their offices.

WORK ENVIRONMENT

The drafter usually works in a well-lighted, air-conditioned, quiet room. This may be a central drafting room where drafters work side by side at large, tilted drawing tables or at CADD workstations. Some drafters work in an individual department, such as engineering, research, or development, where they work alone or with other drafters and with engineers, designers, or scientists. Occasionally, drafters may need to visit other departments or construction sites to consult with engineers or to gain firsthand information. In general, this is a desk job.

Most drafters work a 40-hour week with little overtime. Drafters work at drawing tables or computer stations for long periods of time, doing work that requires undivided concentration, close visual work, and very precise and accurate computations and drawings. There is generally little pressure, but occasionally last-minute design changes or a rush order may create tension or require overtime.

OUTLOOK

The U.S. Department of Labor predicts that employment for drafters in general will grow more slowly than the average for all careers through 2018. Architectural and civil drafters will have the best opportunities, with projected employment growth about as fast as the average for all occupations through 2018. Outsourcing of CADD-related work may reduce employment opportunities for drafters. Increasing use of CADD technology will limit the demand for less skilled drafters, but industrial growth and more complex designs of new products and manufacturing processes will increase the demand for drafting services. In addition, drafters are beginning to increasingly do work traditionally performed by engineers and architects. Nevertheless, job openings will be available as drafters leave the field for other positions or retirement. Opportunities will be best for drafters who have at least two years of postsecondary training and have strong technical skills and significant experience using CADD systems. Employment trends for drafters do fluctuate with the economy, however. During recessions, fewer buildings and manufactured products are designed, which could reduce the need for drafters in architectural, engineering, and manufacturing firms.

FOR MORE INFORMATION

For information on careers in drafting and certification, contact
American Design Drafting Association/American Digital
Design Association
105 East Main Street
Newbern, TN 38059-1526
Tel: 731-627-0802
http://www.adda.org

For news on laws affecting the field and other current topics, contact this union for the drafting community.
International Federation of Professional and Technical Engineers
501 Third Street, NW, Suite 701
Washington, DC 20001-2760
Tel: 202-239-4880
http://www.ifpte.org

Exhibit Designers

QUICK FACTS

School Subjects
Art
English
History

Personal Skills
Communication/ideas
Helping/teaching

Work Environment
Primarily indoors
One location with some travel

Minimum Education Level
Some postsecondary training

Salary Range
$25,150 to $44,660 to
$175,000

Certification or Licensing
None available

Outlook
Faster than the average

DOT
142

GOE
01.04.02

NOC
5243

O*NET-SOC
27-1027.00, 27-1027.02

OVERVIEW

Exhibit designers plan, develop, and produce physical displays for exhibitions at museums and similar institutions. Designers work closely with museum directors, educators, curators, and conservators to create educational exhibits that focus on portions of the museum's collection while maintaining safe environmental conditions for the objects on display. Exhibit designers prepare both temporary and permanent exhibitions for a broad range of museum audiences. There are approximately 10,900 set and exhibit designers working in the United States.

HISTORY

The very first museum prototypes housed books and documents. Museums evolved from these ancient libraries to storage areas for private collections. Eventually, ambitious private collectors began to organize the objects in their collections, first by type (for instance, placing all baskets together), and then by the objects' uniqueness. Private collections became notable if they contained objects that no other collection contained. For as long as unique objects have been cherished, the display of objects has been a necessary practice for satisfying natural human curiosity.

Charles Willson Peale was responsible for opening the first natural history museum intended for public use. As Peale performed all the duties necessary to run his home-based museum, he may also be credited with developing the first exhibit designs in the United States. He exhibited his specimens in natural settings (comparable to modern-day dioramas) to present visitors with contextual information about his collections. As curious visitors began to explore his museum, he realized the need to protect his specimens from environmental damage. He placed the more valuable items in cabinets to protect them from careless hands and reduce the effects of everyday wear and tear. Peale's home museum grew to become the Philadelphia Museum, and with its development came techniques and theories about exhibiting art and cultural artifacts that remain useful today.

THE JOB

Exhibit designers play a key role in helping museums and similar institutions achieve their educational goals. Museums are responsible for providing public access and information about their collections to visitors and scholars. They accomplish this by designing exhibits that display objects and contain contextual information. Because museum visits are interactive experiences, exhibit designers have a responsibility to provide the visiting public with provocative exhibitions that contain visual, emotional, and intellectual components. To achieve this transfer of information, designers must create a nonverbal conversation between exhibits and observers.

The decision to construct a new exhibit is made in collaboration with museum curators, educators, conservators, exhibit designers, and the museum director. After a budget has been set, exhibit designers must meet regularly with curators, educators, and conservators throughout the planning stages. The purpose of each exhibit production is educational, and the team plans each exhibition so that it tells a story. A successful exhibit brings meaning to the objects on display through the use of informative labels (for example, providing a concise overview of early cameras or Egyptian funerary objects), the logical placement of objects, and the construction of display areas that help to place the objects in proper context.

Planning, designing, and producing a new exhibit is a costly as well as a mentally and emotionally challenging project. Exhibit designers must work creatively during the planning and design stages while remaining flexible in their ideas for the exhibition. On many occasions, designers must compromise artistic integrity for the sake of object safety and educational quality. During exhibit installation, designers work closely with the production team, which consists of other designers, technicians, electricians, and carpenters. Lead designers oversee the exhibit installation and attend to last-minute preparations. Most permanent exhibits are planned four years in advance while most temporary exhibits are allowed between six to 18 months for production.

Exhibit designers have additional responsibilities that include researching exhibit topics and new exhibit theories. Designers must also attend conventions of professional associations and contribute to the advancement of their field by writing scholarly articles about new display techniques.

REQUIREMENTS

High School

Exhibit designers, like the majority of museum professionals, need diverse educational backgrounds to perform well in their jobs. Designers must develop their creative and artistic skills and master mathematics courses. At the high school level, take courses in English, history, science, art, and foreign language. These courses will give you general background knowledge you can use to define educational components of exhibitions. Solid geometry, algebra, advanced math, and physics are essential courses for future designers. Exhibit plans must be drawn to scale (often using the metric system) and measurements must be precise. Computer skills are equally necessary as many designers use computer-aided design and drafting technology when planning exhibits. Finally, courses in studio art and drawing will introduce you to the hands-on nature of exhibit work.

Postsecondary Training

Some postsecondary training, including college-level math, art, and design courses, is necessary, and most museums expect candidates for the position of exhibit designer to hold a bachelor's degree. Designers who specialize in a design-related subject and continue their studies in a museum's specialty, such as art, photography, history, or science, have an advantage in being hired by that type of museum.

Those who desire a director position in a museum's design department should consider acquiring an advanced degree.

Other Requirements

Excellent communication skills are essential in this career. Exhibit designers must be able to clearly express their ideas to both museum staff members who collaborate on exhibit projects and to visitors through the display medium. Designing exhibits is mentally challenging and can be physically demanding. Exhibit designers should be artistic, creative, and knowledgeable about preparing safe display environments that accommodate valuable and fragile objects.

EXPLORING

The best way to learn more about exhibit design is to consult with a professional in the field. Contact your local museum, historical society, or related institution to interview and possibly observe a designer at work. Remain informed of the many new challenges and theories that influence an exhibit designer's work. Joining a professional association, reading industry publications such as the American Association of Museum's *Museum* and *Aviso*, or volunteering in a museum or art gallery are all excellent ways to explore this career.

Experience with design in other settings can also contribute to developing the skills needed by exhibit designers. You should consider taking studio classes from a local art guild, offer to design school bulletin boards, or design stage sets for the school drama club or local theater company.

EMPLOYERS

Approximately 10,900 set and exhibit designers are employed in the United States. Museums and private companies that display collections hire exhibit designers. Historical societies, state and federal agencies with archives, and libraries also employ exhibit designers because of their specialized skills in developing thoughtful displays while considering object safety. Exhibit designers may also find work with private design firms as well as exhibition companies that create and distribute both temporary and permanent exhibits throughout the world.

STARTING OUT

Students who wish to become exhibit designers should supplement their design courses with an internship in a museum or a related institution. Some museums offer full- or part-time positions to qualified candidates when they complete their internship hours. Publications such as *Aviso,* which is published monthly, contain classified advertisements for available museum positions. Contacting other professional associations for job listings is also an acceptable method of starting out. Museum positions are highly competitive, and a proven history of experience is invaluable. Keep a portfolio of your design examples to show to potential employers.

ADVANCEMENT

Experienced exhibit designers with appropriate academic credentials and a history of creating educational and visitor-friendly displays are well situated to move into supervisory positions with greater responsibility and design freedom. Exhibit designers may choose to acquire advanced degrees in specialties such as architecture or graphic design in order to achieve the director of exhibitions position. Appropriately educated exhibit designers wishing to move into another area of the museum field may learn to assist conservators, become museum educators, collections managers, curators, or registrars. Exhibit designers who leave museum work are well positioned to seek employment in private design firms.

EARNINGS

Salaries for exhibit designers vary widely depending on the size, type, and location of the institution, as well as the education, expertise, and achievements of the designer. A 2003 salary survey conducted by the Association of Art Museum Directors reported that the average salary of a chief exhibit preparator is roughly $36,000. Earnings ranged from as low as $18,267 to as high as $121,000. The same survey reported that the median salary of an exhibit designer was approximately $50,000, but ranged from as low as $31,000 to as high as $175,000. Some larger or better-funded museums, historical societies, and related institutions pay significantly more, while others may hire on a contractual basis for a predetermined design and installation fee.

The U.S. Department of Labor reports that median annual earnings for set and exhibit designers were $44,660 in 2008. Salaries ranged from less than $25,150 to more than $79,300.

Fringe benefits, including medical and dental insurance, paid vacations and sick leave, and retirement plans, vary according to each employer's policies.

WORK ENVIRONMENT

Exhibit designers typically work 40 hours per week. Continual challenges and strict deadlines make an exhibit designer's work both creative and demanding. Flexibility in working hours may be a requirement of employment as exhibition installment frequently occurs after museum hours when visitors are not present.

Exhibit designers usually have an office or studio in a private area of the museum but often must work on the exhibit floors during design planning, installation, and tear-down periods. Designers must collaborate with curators, museum educators, and conservators throughout the exhibit planning stages to ensure the educational integrity of the exhibition as well as the safety of the objects.

The rewards for designing in a museum environment include a stimulating workplace where the design medium changes continually, the creative application of design expertise, and the satisfaction of educating visitors through the display of artistically and historically significant objects.

OUTLOOK

The *Occupational Outlook Handbook* reports that employment for set and exhibit designers will grow faster than the average for all occupations through 2018. However, there is strong competition for museum jobs, so designers with experience will have an advantage when applying for positions. As museums continue to face tight budgets, museum directors may choose to contract with independent exhibition and design companies to install new exhibits instead of retaining a staff of in-house designers. Private industry and for-profit companies have continued to grow while nonprofit museums and similar institutions may be experiencing a reduction of staff or limited hiring of new employees.

FOR MORE INFORMATION

For information on museum careers, education, and internships, contact
American Association of Museums
1575 Eye Street, NW, Suite 400
Washington, DC 20005-1113
Tel: 202-289-1818
http://www.aam-us.org

For publications and recent news about art museums, contact
Association of Art Museum Directors
120 East 56th Street, Suite 520
New York, NY 10022-3673
Tel: 212-754-8084
http://www.aamd.org

For information on workshops, earnings, employment, and its quarterly journal, contact
New England Museum Association
22 Mill Street, Suite 409
Arlington, MA 02476-4744
Tel: 781-641-0013
http://www.nemanet.org

Fashion Designers

OVERVIEW

Fashion designers create or adapt original designs for clothing for men, women, and children. Most specialize in one particular type of clothing, such as women's dresses or men's suits. Most designers work for textile, apparel, and pattern manufacturers. Some designers are self-employed and develop a clientele of individual customers or manufacturers. Others work for fashion salons, high-fashion department stores, and specialty shops. A few work in the entertainment industry, designing costumes. There are approximately 22,700 fashion designers employed in the United States.

HISTORY

Originally, people wore garments to help them maintain body temperature rather than for style. Clothing usually was handmade at home. Dress design became a profession around the 1600s. Before the invention of the sewing machine in 1846 by Elias Howe, all garments were made by hand. One of the first designers was Rose Bertin, a French milliner (creator of fashion accessories such as hats and cloaks) who dressed Marie Antoinette and influenced women's fashions during the French Revolution.

Women dominated dress design until 1858, when Charles Frederick Worth, an English tailor and couturier of Empress Eugenie, consort of Napoleon III, opened a salon, or fashion house, in Paris. There, he produced designs for actresses and other wealthy clients—the only individuals with enough time and money to have clothing created specifically for them. Worth was the first designer to make garments from fabrics he had selected; until that time, dressmakers had used fabrics provided by patrons. Worth also was the first designer to display his creations on live models. Today, French designers continue to dominate the field. However, the U.S. garment industry has assumed a position of leadership in clothing design and production in the last 40 years; London and Milan also have become important fashion centers.

THE JOB

Fashion designers create designs for almost anything that is a part of the costume of men, women, or children. They design both outer and inner garments, hats, purses, shoes, gloves, costume jewelry, scarves, or beachwear. Some specialize in certain types of clothing, such as bridal gowns or sportswear. People in this profession range from the few top haute couture designers, who produce one-of-a-kind designs for high-fashion houses, to the thousands of designers who create fashions for mass production and sale to millions of Americans. The largest number of fashion designers are followers rather than originators of fashion, adapting high-end styles to meet the desires of the general public. Many fashion designers are self-employed; some work on a freelance basis.

The designer's original idea for a garment is usually sketched. After a rough sketch is created, the designer begins to shape the pattern pieces that make the garment. The pieces are drawn to actual size on paper and cut out of a rough material, often muslin. The muslin pieces are sewn together and fitted on a model. The designer makes modifications in the pattern pieces or other features of the rough mock-up to complete the design. From the rough model, sample garments are made in the fabric that the designer intends to use.

Today's designers are greatly assisted by computer software. Computer-aided designing and computer-aided manufacturing allow for thousands of fashion styles and colors to be stored in a computer and accessed at the touch of a button, largely eliminating the long process of gathering fabrics and styling them into samples.

Sample garments are displayed at a "showing," to which *press representatives* and *buyers* are invited to see the latest designs. Major designers may present large runway shows twice a year to leading retailers and the fashion press for potential publicity and sales. Sample garments may then be mass-produced, displayed by *fashion models,* and shipped to stores where they are available for purchase.

In some companies, designers are involved in every step of the production of a selected line, from the original idea to the completed garments. Many designers prefer to supervise their own workrooms.

Fashion designer Isabel Toledo adjusts the folds on a gown that is part of a retrospective exhibit of her work. *(Kathy Willens, AP Photo)*

Others work with supervisors to solve problems that arise in the production of the garments.

Most manufacturers produce new styles four times each year: spring and summer; fall and winter; vacation wear; and holiday styles. Designers generally are expected to create between 50 and 150 styles for each showing. Their work calendar differs from the actual time of year. They must be working on spring and summer designs during fall and winter, and on fall and winter clothing during the summer.

Designers work cooperatively with the head of their manufacturing firm. They design a line that is consistent with the ideas of their employers. They also work cooperatively with those who do the actual production of the garments and must be able to estimate the cost of a garment. Some company designers produce designs and oversee a workroom staff, which may consist of a head designer, an assistant designer, and one or more sample makers. Designers in large firms may plan and direct the work of one or more assistant designers, select fabrics and trims, and help determine the pricing of the products they design.

Designers spend time in exploration and research, visiting textile manufacturing and sales establishments to learn of the latest fabrics and their uses and capabilities. They must know about fabric, weave, draping qualities, and strength of materials. A good understanding of textiles and their qualities underlies much of designers' work. They browse through stores to see what fashion items the public is buying and which are passed by. They visit museums and art galleries to get ideas about color and design. They go to places where people congregate—theaters, sports events, business and professional meetings, and resorts—and meet with marketing and production workers, salespeople, and clients to discover what people are wearing and to discuss ideas and styles.

Designers also keep abreast of changing styles. If the styles are too different from public taste, customers will reject the designs. If, however, they cling to styles that have been successful in the past, they may find that the taste of buyers has changed dramatically. In either case, it could be equally disastrous for their employers.

There are many opportunities for specialization in fashion designing. The most common specialties are resort wear, bridal wear, and sportswear.

An interesting specialty in fashion designing is costume design, a relatively small field but challenging to those who are interested in combining an interest in stage, film, television, dance, or opera with a talent for clothing design.

REQUIREMENTS

High School

A high school diploma is needed for fashion designing and should include courses that prepare you for more specialized training after graduation. Art, home economics, mathematics, and chemistry all should be included.

Postsecondary Training

An aspiring designer with a total fashion background that includes marketing and other business skills will be favored by employers over a talented person with no knowledge of business procedures. A college degree is recommended, although not required. Graduation from a fashion design school is highly desirable. Employers seek designers who have had courses in mathematics, business, design, sketching, art history, costume history, literature, pattern making, clothing construction, and textiles.

Some colleges offer a four-year degree in fine arts with a major in fashion design. Many reputable schools of fashion design offer a two- or three-year program that offers a diploma or certificate.

Students interested in fashion should take computer-aided design courses, as computers are increasingly being used by designers to better visualize a final product, create prototypes, and reduce design production time and cost. Companies are looking for more than design skills: Many require extensive knowledge and experience with software programs used to produce technical drawings.

Other Requirements

Prospective fashion designers must be artistic and imaginative with a flair for color and clothing coordination. They will need a working knowledge of clothing construction and an eye for trends. They must possess technical aptitudes, problem-solving skills, and the ability to conceptualize in two and three dimensions. Personal qualifications include self-motivation, team spirit, and the ability to handle pressure, deadlines, and long hours. This career also demands energy and a good head for business.

EXPLORING

If you enjoy sewing, you may have taken the first step toward exploring a career in the fashion world. If your skills in garment construction are adequate, the next step may be an attempt at designing and making clothing. Art and design courses will help assess your talent and ability as a creative artist.

If you are able to obtain a summer job in a department or specialty store, you can observe retailing practices and gain some practical insights into the merchandising aspects of the fashion world. Working in a fabric store can provide the opportunity to learn about fabrics and accessories. You may want to visit a garment manufacturer to see fashion employees at work.

You also can attend style shows, visit art galleries, observe clothing worn by fashion leaders, and browse through a variety of stores in which garments are sold. There are many useful books and magazines about fashion. The so-called fashion industry bible is *Women's Wear Daily,* a must read for those who want to be knowledgeable and current in this fast-changing business. To read articles online or for subscription information, visit http://www.wwd.com.

EMPLOYERS

Approximately 22,700 fashion designers are employed in the United States; about 31 percent of designers work for apparel, piece goods, and notions merchants wholesalers; and 13 percent work for apparel manufacturers. Others are self-employed. Many fashion designers find employment with large fashion houses such as Liz Claiborne or Jones New York. Some large manufacturers produce a secondary line of lower-priced designer clothing—Donna Karan's DKNY and Giorgio Armani's Emporio, for example. In the United States, New York City, San Francisco, and Los Angeles are major fashion centers and positions may be found in both large and small companies. Work also may be found in Chicago and other cities, although not as many jobs are available in these locations.

A few fashion designers work for high-fashion firms, but these positions are difficult to come by and competition is very strong. An aspiring designer may have more options in specialized areas of fashion such as sportswear, sleepwear, children's clothing, or accessories.

Other areas for aspiring fashion designers to explore are home fashions such as bed and bath linens, draperies, and rugs or carpeting. Positions also can be found with pattern manufacturers. Some fashion designers work on a freelance basis, contracting with manufacturers or individuals.

An easy way to learn about manufacturers is to visit a department or specialty store and examine labels and tags on merchandise of interest. In addition to major department stores, retailers such as Target carry a variety of manufacturers' lines.

STARTING OUT

Few people begin their careers as fashion designers. Well-trained college graduates often begin as *assistant designers*. Assistants must prove their ability before being entrusted with the responsible job of the designer. Many young people find that assistant designer jobs are difficult to locate, so they accept beginning jobs in the workroom where they spend time cutting or constructing garments.

Fashion design school graduates may receive placement information from their school or college career services offices. Approaching stores and manufacturers directly is another way to secure a beginning position. However, you will be more successful if you have contacts in the industry through previous summer or part-time work.

ADVANCEMENT

Advancement in fashion designing varies a great deal. There is much movement from firm to firm, and vacancies occur frequently. Aspiring designers should create, collect, and continuously update their portfolios of designs and look for opportunities to show their work to employers. Beginners may work as cutting assistants or assistant designers. From these entry-level positions, the fashion designer's career path may lead to positions as an assistant technical designer, pattern company designer, designer, and head designer. Those who grow with a company may design less and take on more operational responsibilities.

Designers may choose to move into a business or merchandising position where they direct lines, set prices, supervise production, and work directly with buyers. After years of work, top designers may become partners in the design or apparel firms for which they work. Others may open their own retail clothing stores. A designer may want to work for firms that offer increasing design responsibility and fewer restrictions to become established as a house designer or eventually as an independent-name designer.

EARNINGS

Fashion designers earned an average salary of $61,160 in 2008, according to the U.S. Department of Labor. The lowest paid 10 percent earned less than $32,150; the highest paid 10 percent earned more than $124,780. A few highly skilled and well-known designers in top firms have annual incomes of more than $150,000. Top fashion designers who have successful lines of clothing can earn bonuses that bring their annual incomes into the millions. As designers become well known, they are usually offered a share of the ownership of the company for which they design. Their ownership percentage increases with their reputation.

Theatrical designers usually work on a contract basis. Although the compensation for the total contract is usually good, there may be long periods of idleness between contracts. The annual incomes for theatrical designers usually are not as great as those of fashion designers, although while they are working they may be making more than $1,000 per week.

Fashion designers who work for a company usually receive benefits such as vacation days, sick leave, health and life insurance, and a savings and pension program. Self-employed designers must provide their own benefits.

WORK ENVIRONMENT

Fashion design is competitive and stressful, but often exciting and glamorous. Many designers work in cluttered and noisy surroundings. Their work environment may consist of a large room with long tables for cutting out patterns or garments. There may be only one or two other people working in the room, or there may be several other workers. Many designers travel a great deal for showings and conferences. They may spend time in stores or shops looking at clothing that has been manufactured by competitors.

Most designers work a 40-hour week, but they may have to work more during rush periods. Styles previewed for one season require a great amount of work during the weeks and months before a show. The work pace is usually hectic as pressure builds before collection showings.

OUTLOOK

Designers are key people in the garment industry, yet relatively few of them are needed to make employment possible for thousands of people in other apparel occupations. There are approximately 22,700 fashion designers in the United States, which represents a tiny percentage of the garment industry. Some designers work only for the high-priced custom trade, some for the mass market, and some on exclusive designs that will be made for only one person. Many designers are employed by manufacturers of paper patterns.

According to the *Occupational Outlook Handbook,* employment of designers is expected to experience little or no change compared to the average for all occupations through 2018. Good designers will always be needed, although not in great numbers. However, increasing populations and growing personal incomes are expected to spur the demand for fashion designer—especially those who design mass market clothing sold in department stores and retail chain stores.

Some fashion designers enjoy high pay and prestige. Those at the top of their profession rarely leave their positions. Therefore, opportunities for newcomers are limited. There always will be more people hoping to break into the field than there are available jobs. Experience working with computer-aided design programs is increasingly important to employers and can help to distinguish a qualified job candidate from the rest of his or her competition. Employment prospects may be better in specialized areas, such as children's clothing. Additionally, openings are more readily available for assistant designers.

FOR MORE INFORMATION

For industry information, contact
Council of Fashion Designers of America
1412 Broadway, Suite 2006
New York, NY 10018-9250
http://www.cfda.com

Those interested in creating men's fashions should check out the CTDA Web site for business and training information.

Custom Tailors and Designers Association (CTDA)
42732 Ridgeway Drive
Broadlands, VA 20148-4558
Tel: 888-248-2832
http://www.ctda.com

For information about this school, programs, and an application, contact

Fashion Institute of Technology
227 West 27th Street
New York, NY 10001-5992
Tel: 212-217-7999
http://www.fitnyc.edu

Fashion Group International is a nonprofit association of more than 6,000 professionals in the fashion, apparel, accessories, beauty, and home industries. Visit its Web site for information on college student membership, career counseling resources, and student career days.

Fashion Group International
8 West 40th Street, 7th Floor
New York, NY 10018-2276
Tel: 212-302-5511
http://www.fgi.org

For industry information, contact

International Association of Clothing Designers & Executives
835 Northwest 36th Terrace
Oklahoma City, OK 73118-7104
Tel: 405-602-8037
http://www.iacde.com

For a list of accredited schools, contact

National Association of Schools of Art and Design
11250 Roger Bacon Drive, Suite 21
Reston, VA 20190 -5248
Tel: 703-437-0700
E-mail: info@arts-accredit.org
http://nasad.arts-accredit.org

Florists

OVERVIEW

Florists arrange live or cut flowers, potted plants, foliage, or other decorative items according to basic design principles to make eye-pleasing creations. Designers make such arrangements for birthdays, weddings, funerals, or other occasions. They are employed by local flower shops or larger national chains, grocery stores, or established at-home businesses. Florists are also known as *floral designers*. There are approximately 76,100 floral design workers employed in the United States.

HISTORY

Flowers have been used for thousands of years as decoration, personal adornment, or for religious purposes. Ancient Egyptians used flowers to honor their many gods and goddesses. Flowers were arranged in low bowls in an orderly, repetitive pattern—flower, bud, foliage, and so on. Special spouted vases were also used to hold flowers. Lotus flowers, also called water lilies, were Egyptian favorites. They came to symbolize sacredness and were associated with Isis, the Egyptian nature goddess. Flowers were sometimes used as decorations for the body, collar, and hair.

Flowers were fashioned into elaborate wreaths and garlands by the ancient Greeks. The best wreathmakers were often commissioned by wealthy Greeks to make wreaths for gifts, awards, or decoration. Chaplets, special wreaths for the head, were especially popular. Cornucopia, a horn-shaped container still used today, were filled with arrangements of flowers, fruits, and vegetables. Flowers arranged into wreaths

QUICK FACTS

School Subjects
Agriculture
Art
Business

Personal Skills
Artistic
Following instructions
Leadership/management

Work Environment
Primarily indoors
Primarily one location

Minimum Education Level
High school diploma

Salary Range
$16,210 to $23,230 to $35,010+

Certification or Licensing
Recommended (certification)
Required by certain states (licensing)

Outlook
Decline

DOT
142

GOE
01.04.02

NOC
0621

O*NET-SOC
27-1023.00

and garlands were also popular during the Roman period and well through to the Middle Ages.

The Victorian era saw great developments in the art of floral design. There was enormous enthusiasm for flowers, plants, and gardens; the most cultured young ladies were often schooled in the art of flower arrangement. Rules were first established regarding function and design. Magazines and books about floral arrangement were also published during this time. Proper Victorian ladies often had fresh nosegays, or tussie-mussies, a hand-held arrangement of tightly knotted flowers, for sentimental reasons, if not to freshen the air. Posy holders, fancy carriers for these small floral arrangements, came into fashion. Some were made of ivory, glass, or mother-of-pearl, and were elaborately decorated with jewels or etchings. Flowers were also made into small arrangements and tucked into a lady's décolletage inside aptly named containers, bosom bottles.

Ikebana, the Japanese art of floral arrangement that was created in the sixth century, has been a principal influence on formal flower arrangement design. Its popularity still continues today. In the 1950s, free-form expression developed, incorporating pieces of driftwood and figurines within arrangements of flowers and live plants.

Floral traditions of the past still have an impact on us today. It is still fashionable to mark special occasions with flowers, be it an anniversary, wedding, or birthday. People continue to use flowers to commemorate the dead. Today's floral arrangements reflect the current style, trends, and tastes. The best floral designers will follow the developing fashions and creatively adapt them to their arrangements.

THE JOB

From simple birthday bouquets to lavish wedding arrangements, floral designers define a sentiment, a mood, or make an impression, using flowers as their medium of expression. Along with live flowers, designers may use silk flowers or foliage, fresh fruit, and twigs or incorporate decorative items such as candles, balloons, ribbons, and stuffed animals to their arrangements. Good equipment—foam, wire, wooden or plastic picks, shears, florist's knife, tape, and a variety of containers—is essential. Techniques such as wiring flower stems or shading the tips of blooms with paint or glitter are often used to give floral arrangements a finished look. Familiarity with different species of flowers and plants, as well as creativity and knowledge of the elements of design are what distinguish a good floral designer.

Floral designers are fortunate to have a number of employment paths from which to choose. Some designers are employed at flower shops, while some opt to work independently. Aurora Gagni, owner of Floral Elegance, is one such entrepreneur. A registered nurse by training but creative by nature, Gagni always enjoyed making crafts. "I would see a picture of a flower arrangement in a magazine and try to duplicate it," she says, "but I would always add and experiment and make it my own creation." Gagni made floral arrangements, wreaths, and displays for family, friends, and coworkers, who in turn would spread word of her abilities. "At one point, I found myself giving bow-making lessons at work!" In time, Gagni had a steady and growing number of customers who relied on her skills.

What persuaded Gagni to give up nursing and go into business for herself? "My kids!" she answers. Indeed, this job perk is an attractive one, especially for someone juggling a career with family. Gagni conducts her business almost entirely from her home, and is available for the "many little things"—driving to and from sports events, delivering forgotten lunch boxes, and, of course, homework.

Gagni tackles a variety of floral requests, but weddings are her specialty. While a typical wedding day lasts a few hours, the planning stage can take months. "Usually, the bride and groom look at my book," Gagni says, "and decide if they like my work." If so, the contract is "closed"—the contract agreement is signed, a budget is set, and a down payment is made—several months before the wedding day. Soon after, designs are made, keeping the budget in mind. Many brides wish for orchids with a carnation budget. "I try to accommodate what type of flower, or color, or look the customer wants," Gagni explains, sometimes making alternate suggestions, especially if price is an issue, or if the flower is difficult to obtain. Gagni orders necessary supplies weeks in advance and scouts for upcoming sales. She notifies her floral wholesalers in advance of any flowers that are seasonal or difficult to obtain. Also, she visits the church and reception hall to check on details such as size, location, and any restrictions. The quickest route to both destinations is also mapped out to ensure prompt delivery of the flowers.

Gagni periodically checks in with the bride about any last-minute changes. Oftentimes, more corsages or more banquet table centerpieces are needed to accommodate extra guests. Bows are tied and secured with wire about two weeks before the wedding. Three days before the wedding, flowers are picked and kept fresh in buckets of water treated with floral preservatives. The actual arranging, done in Gagni's basement, is begun the night before the wedding—bricks of floral foam, treated with water and preservatives, keep the flow-

The owner of a floral design shop puts the finishing touches on an arrangement. (*Matt Detrich, AP Photo*/The Indianapolis Star)

ers in place. Bouquets and corsages are delivered to the bride's home on the morning of the wedding; and ribbons, flower arrangements, and corsages for the groom's party, are brought to the location of the ceremony. Gagni then goes to the hall to set up for the reception. Final touch-ups are given to table centerpieces, the head table is decorated, and the last details are tackled.

Gagni hires additional help for large contracts, especially to assist with the final arrangements. Her children also help when needed, and her husband is her unofficial delivery driver.

Most retail floral businesses keep a relatively small staff. Sales workers help customers place their orders; they also take care of phone orders. Drivers are hired to make deliveries. Sometimes assistant designers are employed.

REQUIREMENTS

High School
Take art and design classes while in high school. After all, "creativity" is an important buzzword in this industry. Biology classes would be helpful in learning about plants and flowers. Do you have aspirations of owning a flower establishment? Sign up for business-related courses and computer classes—they will help make you a better entrepreneur.

Postsecondary Training

In the past, floral designers learned their craft on the job, usually working as an assistant or apprentice to an experienced designer. Most designers today, however, pursue advanced education resulting in a certificate or degree. While this education is not mandatory in the industry, it does give candidates an advantage when they apply for design positions. There are numerous universities that offer degrees in floriculture and horticulture, as well as community colleges and independent schools that offer certification in floral design.

Programs vary from school to school, lasting anywhere from days to years depending on the type of degree or certificate. For example, the American Floral Art School (http://www.americanfloralartschool.com), a state-approved and licensed vocational school in Chicago, offers courses in modern floral design, with class schedules from one to three weeks. The curriculum includes the fundamentals of artistic floral design, general instruction in picking or wiring, tinting, and arranging flowers, different types of arrangements and their containers, fashion flowers and wedding flowers, and flower shop management. When you are choosing a school to attend, consider the course offerings as well as your career goals. For example, the Boston-based Rittners School of Floral Design (http://www.floralschool.com) offers classes that emphasize floral business skills, a must if you plan on starting your own shop. Some distance education is also available. The Society of American Florists (http://www.safnow.org) has an online learning center through which various courses are offered.

Certification or Licensing

The American Institute of Floral Designers (AIFD) offers the accredited in floral design designation to applicants who complete an open-book test and participate in evaluation sessions in which they create designs in the following categories: Sympathy Design, Arrangement, Wedding, Flowers to Wear, and Duplicate (recreating a sample design). Contact the AIFD for more information.

Owners of floral shops in some states may need to apply for a business license. Individual states or communities may have zoning codes or other regulations specifying what type of business can be located in a particular area. Check with your state's chamber of commerce or department of revenue for more information on obtaining a license.

Other Requirements

Most people don't wake up one morning and decide to become a floral designer. If you don't have creative and artistic inclinations, you're already a step behind the rest. A good floral designer enjoys and understands plants and flowers, and can visualize a creation from the very first daffodil. Are you able to work well under pressure and deadlines, and effectively deal with vendors or wholesalers? These are daily requirements of the job. Also, be prepared to greet and accommodate all types of customers, from impatient grooms to nervous brides to grieving families. A compassionate and patient personality will help you go far in this field.

EXPLORING

Considering a future in floral design? Now is the best time to determine if this career is the right one for you. As a high school student without experience, it's doubtful you'll be hired as a floral designer; but working as a cashier, flower delivery person, or an assistant is a great way to break into the industry.

What about taking some classes to test your talent? Michaels, a national arts and crafts retailer, offers floral design workshops. Look for similar workshops in your area. Park district programs also have design classes, especially during the holiday seasons. Such programs are relatively inexpensive—most times the fee is just enough to cover materials used in class.

Learn the industry firsthand—why not spend a day at work with a floral designer? Explain your interest to your local florist and ask if he or she would be willing to let you observe.

EMPLOYERS

Approximately 76,100 floral designers are employed in the United States. Small, independently owned flower shops employ about 50 percent of florists. Large, national chains, such as Teleflora and FTD, supply additional jobs. Flower departments, now a staple in larger grocery stores, employ about 12 percent of floral designers. Other floral designers are self-employed.

STARTING OUT

Some floral designers get their start by working as assistant designers. Others, especially if they are certified, may be hired as floral designers. Experienced designers may concentrate in a certain area, such as weddings, and become wedding specialists.

Aurora Gagni needed to apply for a tax identification number before she officially "opened" her business. This number is necessary to establish accounts with wholesalers and greenhouses, as well as for tax purposes. It would be wise to consult with business or legal experts regarding income tax issues, promotion and advertising, and other matters dealing with operating your own business.

Professionals in floral design maintain a portfolio of their best designs. A portfolio is useful when applying for membership in floral associations, classes, and when wooing potential clients.

ADVANCEMENT

Advancement in this field depends on the interest of the individual. Some floral designers are content to work at small local shops, especially if they have created a name for themselves in the area they serve. Others decide to try employment with larger national chains such as Teleflora, or 1-800-FLOWERS. Superstore grocery chains now boast full-service floral departments, creating many job opportunities for designers.

Do you possess an entrepreneurial nature? Maybe owning a floral business—either based in your home or established in the middle of your town's business district—is in your future. Still other options include entering the field of landscape design; interior landscaping for offices, shopping centers, and hotels; or a large floral design specialty. Imagine working on a float for Pasadena's Tournament of Roses Parade.

Many of Aurora Gagni's contracts are for weddings, so it makes sense that her business branches out accordingly. Party favors, cake toppers, and the veil and cord—elements unique in many ethnic wedding ceremonies—are some items Gagni customizes for her clients.

EARNINGS

Experience counts for a lot when it comes to a designer's salary. Geographic location also plays a part in salary differences. Floral designers on the East and West Coasts traditionally enjoy higher than average salaries, compared to floral designers in other parts of the United States. Stores located in large urban areas tend to have higher annual sales than those in rural areas, resulting in higher pay for their employees.

Florists had median annual earnings of $23,230 in 2008, according to the U.S. Department of Labor (DOL). Well-established floral designers with a steady customer base can earn more than $35,010 annually. Less experienced florists may earn less than $16,210 annually. The DOL also reports that florists employed in grocery stores earned mean annual salaries of $26,010 in 2008.

Depending on the store, designers may be offered sick leave and vacation time, health and life insurance, as well as other benefits.

WORK ENVIRONMENT

Flowers can be purchased almost anywhere, from small strip-mall flower shops to large national chains to the neighborhood grocery store. This availability means that floral designers can work almost anywhere—from remote, rural areas to busy cities.

Retail floral designers can expect to have comfortable work surroundings. Most floral shops are cool, clean, and well decorated to help attract customers. Glass refrigerators filled with fresh flowers, live plants and flower arrangements, and arts and crafts are typical items in any flower shop. Work stations for making floral pieces are usually found in the back of the store, along with supplies, containers, and necessary equipment.

Expect to spend the majority of the time on your feet—either standing while working on an arrangement, consulting with customers regarding types of flowers, or on a flower-buying expedition. Most retail-based designers work a normal eight-hour workday with a day off during the week. Weekends are especially busy (often because of weddings) and holidays notoriously so. Christmas, Mother's Day, and Valentine's Day are peak times for floral orders. Long work hours are the norm during these times to accommodate the heavy demand for flowers.

Most designers, if contracted to work a wedding, will travel to the church or the banquet hall to make sure the church arrangements or the table arrangements are properly set up.

OUTLOOK

Employment in floral design is expected to decline through 2018, according to the U.S. Department of Labor. Despite this prediction, there should continue to be good opportunities as many florists leave the field for design positions that offer higher pay and more opportunities for advancement (advancement in this career is limited for florists who do not pursue management positions or open their own business). The emergence of full-service floral departments in grocery stores, as well as opportunities in Internet floral shops, have also contributed to job availability. Floral experts who are able to create exciting and original designs will be in high demand. Certified designers may have an edge for the best jobs.

A growing population with large disposable incomes is good news for this industry. Sending flowers to mark an occasion is an old tradition that still has impact today. The increase in lavish weddings and other events, as well as the growing demand for high-quality artificial flower decorations in homes and businesses, will create new jobs for florists.

FOR MORE INFORMATION

For fun and interesting information about flowers, visit the SAF's Aboutflowers.com Web site.
Aboutflowers.com
http://www.aboutflowers.com

For information on accreditation, student chapters, and scholarships available through the AIFD Foundation, contact
American Institute of Floral Designers (AIFD)
720 Light Street
Baltimore, MD 21230-3850
Tel: 410-752-3318
E-mail: aifd@assnhqtrs.com
http://www.aifd.org

For education information, including online courses offered through the SAF, contact
Society of American Florists (SAF)
1601 Duke Street
Alexandria, VA 22314-3406
Tel: 703-836-8700
E-mail: info@safnow.org
http://www.safnow.org

Furniture Designers

QUICK FACTS

School Subjects
Art
Mathematics
Technical/shop

Personal Skills
Artistic
Communication/ideas

Work Environment
Primarily indoors
Primarily one location

Minimum Education Level
Bachelor's degree

Salary Range
$31,400 to $57,350 to
$110,000+

Certification or Licensing
None available

Outlook
About as fast as the average

DOT
142

GOE
01.04.02

NOC
2252

O*NET-SOC
27-1021.00

OVERVIEW

Furniture designers develop concepts for building furnishings like chairs, tables, and couches. They work closely with their clients to get a thorough understanding of what kind of product is needed.

Furniture designers may work for a company that specifically builds furniture or for a large design firm that is contracted by furniture manufacturers. Furniture designers spend most of their time in an office working on ideas but also spend time meeting with clients.

HISTORY

The oldest furniture still intact today is Egyptian, from the fourth to the sixth dynasties (about 2680–2255 B.C.). Many of the construction techniques used by Egyptian craft workers are still used commonly today. Larger pieces, such as tables and chairs, were built using mortise-and-tenon joinery, and small chests and boxes were dovetailed together. Artisans in this period used design elements that recur throughout history, such as carving table and chair legs designed in the likeness of animal legs.

During every period in history from early Egyptian times until now, design has ranged from the simple and purely functional to the ornate and intricately crafted. However, civilization has tended to preserve furniture that is more intricate. From a historical point of view, this is fortunate. Ornate craftwork tells more about a period than simple design does because it evolves to reflect artistic concepts and fashions. On the other hand, if you compared a simple farmer's table from 1700 B.C. with a farmer's table from 1700 A.D., you would probably find more similarities than differences.

Evidence of design and construction practices in some cultures is mostly limited to what we can observe in surviving paintings, sculpture, mosaics, and other graphic representations. Not many actual pieces remain from the Mesopotamians, the Minoans (of the Aegean Islands), the ancient Greeks, or from the Byzantine era (the mid- to late centuries of the first millennium A.D.).

In most cultures, artisans have tended to build furniture to mirror elements and styles of architecture. In 15th-century Gothic design, architectural themes such as arches, line tracery, columns, and leaf patterns began to appear in furniture. During the French Renaissance, the architectural style of Jacques du Cerceau, which featured intricate patterns made up of classical elements, was translated into furniture design. From the 1890s until 1910, European architects and artisans inspired by the Art Nouveau movement infused their work with suggestions of shapes in nature and an impression of movement. The Belgian architects Henri van de Velde and Victor Horta created furnishings that echoed the organic curvature prominent in the buildings they designed.

During the 18th and 19th centuries, a wave of revivalism unearthed earlier styles of design. In the mid-1700s, designers in Europe (notably, England and France) began using ancient Greek and Roman ideas, giving rise to Neoclassicism. During this time, artisans used basic geometric shapes in furniture. Surfaces were often variations of the circle or the square, and legs were built with unbroken, tapering lines. Ornament often contained style elements seen in Greco-Roman columns. Later, in the mid-1800s, the Gothic revival saw the return of Gothic architectural themes in furniture design (e.g., pointed arches, columns, and "linenfold," an ornamental carving style mimicking the folds of hanging fabric). In the 1860s, Renaissance revival brought back pieces built with straight lines and decorated with inlaid patterns.

During most of the history of furniture design, each period has been characterized by a single or very few styles and designers (for example, Gustav Stickley was famous in the Arts and Crafts movement of the late 19th and early 20th centuries). Things are very different today. Designers employ hundreds of styles, from the antique to the high tech. Some of the best designers draw from multiple influences in creating their work.

THE JOB

Furniture design encompasses a variety of skills and disciplines, including history, art, mathematics, drafting, ergonomics, interior design, and carpentry. Furniture designers generate ideas for new pieces or lines of furniture. They usually start with a graphic representation (rough sketches) of the piece to be built and then they build an actual model out of wood or foam core to view the piece in three-dimensional space. Once the model is completed, a prototype is built to the correct size using actual materials. After the prototype is approved, it goes into production, which could involve one carpenter for a custom-designed piece, or a huge factory that mass produces a variety of pieces.

Furniture designers sit at a drawing board making technical drawings, usually using CAD (computer-aided design/drafting) software to illustrate their ideas. They must consider the intended function of the piece, its form, its style, and its environment. The furniture may be a reproduction of a period piece or influenced by an earlier style, or it may be a completely original design. Other considerations include materials, cost, manufacturing processes, and the manufacturing time.

Communication is an important part of the design process. Furniture designers must understand the clients' or employers' demands and be able to translate them into a working model. They must then communicate their ideas to builders and manufacturers to explain materials, shapes, patterns, and construction details. Production of furniture is a complex process that usually involves several people. Engineers, carpenters, assemblers, finishers, accountants, salespeople, marketers, and shippers are all part of the team.

Furniture designers who work on their own or for small companies may be involved in the actual construction process in addition to developing designs. They might use such power tools as a table saw, wood lathe, router, joiner/planer, bandsaw, grinders, and sanders, as well as a variety of hand tools. At a larger company, a designer is more likely to be assigned to one function, perhaps technical drawing or building a prototype.

REQUIREMENTS

High School

Art classes are fundamental to your training as a designer. Drawing and sketching classes will help you to get ideas down fast, and sculpture classes will encourage you to think about 3-D objects. A drafting course is also essential. Manual drafting will teach you how to make a technical drawing of a 3-D object, and, in turn, help you to visualize an object by looking at a 2-D drawing. Take shop courses to learn about woodworking and metal fabrication/welding, because wood and metal are among the most common materials used in contemporary furniture building.

Mathematics courses, including algebra, geometry, and trigonometry are necessary. Computer science is beneficial, especially if you have an opportunity to learn CAD software.

Postsecondary Training

In general, a bachelor's degree is required for entry-level positions. Colleges such as the Rhode Island School of Design and the Savannah College of Art and Design have furniture design programs at both the undergraduate and graduate levels. (See contact information at the end of this article.) Also, because it is common now for small furniture manufacturers to contract industrial design firms for their designs, consider schools that have industrial design programs that will allow you to concentrate on furniture design. Of the approximately 300 public and private colleges, universities, and other postsecondary schools offering programs in art and design that are accredited by the National Association of Schools of Art and Design, 40 offer bachelor's degrees in industrial design.

In a design program, early classes will focus on the fundamentals of 2-D and 3-D design. Studio classes give you hands-on experience with wood, power and hand tools, welding and metal fabrication, upholstery techniques, and molding plastics. Design history teaches you how craftspeople and artisans have designed furniture in the past and how past styles influence design today.

Most programs help you assemble a portfolio of work and include an internship segment, in which faculty will help you find a working position with a professional for one or more semesters.

Other Requirements

Furniture designers need artistic ability and must be able to visualize and work in three dimensions. Aside from being creative, you should be able to work well both independently and as part of a team. It helps to be persistent and tough-minded to accept criticism of your designs. Good verbal communication skills will help you communicate with clients, builders, and production workers.

EXPLORING

To investigate your interest in designing furniture, try to design a chair, bookcase, or table. Make rough sketches. If you haven't had any exposure to technical drawing, find a book that describes drafting techniques and buy or borrow the basic tools (vellum, drafting pencils, architect's scale). Try to make a detailed drawing to scale.

After completing your sketch, try building it. Make arrangements with a shop instructor to use the tools at your school. You may have to find the materials yourself. Find out how well your design builds, holds together, and functions.

Get in the habit of looking at manufactured objects. Anything that is built began with a design. Look at pieces as a whole and at the details, and decide what you like and dislike about the design.

Visit local companies that manufacture and/or design furniture. You may be able to work part time or as a volunteer in exchange for learning about the furniture business.

EMPLOYERS

Some of the largest and most established employers of furniture designers in this country are located in the Midwest. Steelcase is located in Grand Rapids, Michigan; Herman Miller is in Zeeland, Michigan; and Knoll is in East Greenville, Pennsylvania. These companies tend to be selective, so you'll probably need a bachelor's degree in design, a few years of experience, and a professional portfolio to get an interview.

There are many smaller companies in cities throughout the United States that design and manufacture their own lines of furniture. They are more likely to hire designers who can perform other functions as well, such as marketing or production.

Industrial design (ID) firms hire people with backgrounds in furniture design. Furniture manufacturers that are too small to have their own design departments sometimes contract ID firms to create concepts for them. The reverse is true as well; large design firms may create designs and contract builders who have the specific facilities and expertise to create what's needed.

Many furniture designers work on a freelance basis. Some develop their own designs and try to sell them to manufacturers, while others are hired by manufacturers to develop designs according to their needs.

STARTING OUT

Probably the most difficult way to get work in this field is to call a firm or a company cold. If you don't have contacts, check with furniture design associations because they often collect job listings.

If you complete a four-year program in furniture design, your instructors and professors will likely be able to put you in touch with numerous professional contacts. Some internships can lead to full-time positions upon graduation.

Some designers start out as woodworkers or craftworkers. After working in a cabinet or furniture shop for a few years, you may wish to start up your own custom furniture business.

ADVANCEMENT

College graduates can start as *junior designers* for companies that make furniture on a small scale. They may begin by building prototypes in the shop. With some experience, they may begin to work in CAD on company designs. As they gain credibility and experience, designers can advance to a management position, in which they spend most of their time communicating with clients. After several years, they may qualify for a senior designer position with a larger manufacturer.

Another way to advance in this career is to start a business or work as a freelance designer, creating original concepts for furniture, which can be custom built or sold to manufacturers.

EARNINGS

Some furniture designers are employed as industrial designers. According to the U.S. Department of Labor, the median annual salary for commercial and industrial designers was $57,350 in 2008. The lowest paid 10 percent earned less than $31,400 and the highest paid 10 percent earned more than $97,700. Designers in managerial or executive positions had higher salaries of more than $110,000.

Benefits for furniture design positions with established firms or manufacturers include health insurance, paid vacation, and sick leave.

WORK ENVIRONMENT

Furniture designers spend a great deal of time in an office working on sketches and technical drawings. They also have to meet with clients on a regular basis. Some work takes place in manufacturing facilities, from a small woodshop to the factory floor of a $2 billion operation. Designers must communicate regularly with builders and production workers to make sure they understand the process, the materials, and the finishes.

Furniture designers working for large companies are more likely to work a regular 40-hour workweek. In smaller companies, they may be required to work extra hours during peak production periods. Design work can be intense and stressful with constant pressure to come up with new ideas.

OUTLOOK

The U.S. Department of Labor predicts that employment for commercial and industrial designers will grow about as fast as the average for all careers through 2018. Openings will result from growth in the field as well as the need to replace designers who leave the industry. Demand for furniture designers should remain strong because a growing number of consumers are concerned with purchasing furniture that is not just utilitarian but also fashionable and stylish.

Trade has become more global, and there are more markets available to U.S. manufacturers. Furniture trade in the United States now competes with that of Europe. The big furniture companies are getting bigger, and they will hire new staff designers, or contract them as freelancers. This growth is happening as consumers are able to afford to furnish their homes the way they want and are becoming more design conscious. This trend is evidenced by the popularity of television shows such as those on the Home & Garden Television (HGTV) cable network and design-oriented magazines like *Metropolitan Home* or *Better Homes & Gardens*.

Freelancers who sell designs to companies that manufacture inexpensive furniture on a large scale can collect royalties based on sales of the product. There is a growing trend among collectors in buying "one-off" (that is, unique) pieces of furniture and limited-production furniture. If your interest is in designing unusual work with an emphasis on beauty and artistry, this collecting trend might work to your advantage.

FOR MORE INFORMATION

For information on the field, educational programs, and other resources, contact
The Furniture Society
111 Grovewood Road
Asheville, NC 28804-2858
Tel: 828-255-1949
E-mail: info@furnituresociety.org
http://www.furnituresociety.org

Visit the education section of the IDSA Web site to read the career brochure Getting an Industrial Design Job, *find a listing of undergraduate and graduate ID programs, obtain information on scholarships and competitions, and more.*
Industrial Designers Society of America (IDSA)
45195 Business Court, Suite 250

Dulles, VA 20166-6717
Tel: 703-707-6000
http://www.idsa.org

For information about accredited schools in art, design, and industrial design, contact
National Association of Schools of Art and Design
11250 Roger Bacon Drive, Suite 21
Reston, VA 20190-5248
Tel: 703-437-0700
E-mail: info@arts-accredit.org
http://nasad.arts-accredit.org

These colleges prepare students for various careers in art and design fields, including furniture design. To read degree requirements typical for the furniture design field, visit the following Web sites:
Rhode Island School of Design
Two College Street
Providence, RI 02903 -2717
Tel: 401-454-6100
E-mail: admissions@risd.edu
http://www.risd.edu

Savannah College of Art and Design
PO Box 2072
Savannah, GA 31402-2072
Tel: 800-869-7223
http://www.scad.edu

Graphic Designers

QUICK FACTS

School Subjects
Art
Computer science

Personal Skills
Artistic
Communication/ideas

Work Environment
Primarily indoors
Primarily one location

Minimum Education Level
Bachelor's degree

Salary Range
$26,110 to $42,400 to
$100,000+

Certification or Licensing
None available

Outlook
About as fast as the average

DOT
141

GOE
01.04.02

NOC
5241

O*NET-SOC
27-1024.00

OVERVIEW

Graphic designers are practical artists whose creations are intended to express ideas, convey information, or draw attention to a product. They design a wide variety of materials including advertisements, marketing materials, displays, packaging, signs, computer graphics and games, book and magazine covers and interiors, animated characters, Web pages, interactive media, and company logos to fit the needs and preferences of their various clients. There are approximately 286,100 graphic designers employed in the United States.

HISTORY

The challenge of combining beauty, function, and technology in whatever form has preoccupied artisans throughout history. Graphic design work has been used to create products and promote commerce for as long as people have used symbols, pictures, and typography to communicate ideas.

Graphic design grew alongside the growth of print media (newspapers, magazines, catalogs, and advertising). Typically, the graphic designer would sketch several rough drafts of the layout of pictures and words. After one of the drafts was approved, the designer would complete a final layout including detailed type and artwork specifications. The words were sent to a typesetter and the artwork assigned to an illustrator. When the final pieces were returned, the designer or a keyline and paste-up artist would adhere them with rubber cement or wax to an illustration board. Different colored items were placed on acetate overlays. This camera-ready art was now ready to be sent to a printer for photographing and reproduction.

72

Computer technology has revolutionized the way many graphic designers do their work. Today it is possible to be a successful graphic designer even if you can't draw more than simple stick figures. Graphic designers are now able to draw, color, and revise the many different images they work with using computers. They can choose typefaces, size type, and place images without having to manually align them on the page using a T square and triangle. Computer graphics enable graphic designers to work more quickly, since details like size, shape, and color are easy to change.

Graphics design software programs are continually revised and improved, moving more and more design work from the artist's table to the computer mousepad and graphics tablet. They are increasingly being called on to develop content for Web pages, multimedia projects, and interactive media.

THE JOB

Graphic designers are not primarily fine artists, although they may be highly skilled at drawing or painting. Most designs commissioned to graphic designers involve both artwork and copy (words). Thus, the designer must not only be familiar with the wide range of art media (photography, drawing, painting, collage, etc.) and styles, but he or she must also be familiar with a wide range of typefaces and know how to manipulate them for the right effect. Because design tends to change in a similar way to fashion, designers must keep up to date with the latest trends. At the same time, they must be well grounded in more traditional, classic designs.

Graphic designers can work as *in-house designers* for a particular company, as *staff designers* for a graphic design firm, or as *freelance designers* working for themselves. Some designers specialize in designing advertising materials or packaging. Others focus on corporate identity materials such as company stationery and logos. Some work mainly for publishers, designing book and magazine covers and page layouts. Some work in the area of computer graphics, creating still or animated graphics for computer software, videos, or motion pictures. A highly specialized type of graphic designer, the *environmental graphic designer,* designs large outdoor signs. Depending on the project's requirements, many graphic designers work exclusively on the computer, while others may use both the computer and drawings or paintings created by hand.

Whatever the specialty and whatever their medium, all graphic designers take a similar approach to a project, whether it is for an entirely new design or for a variation on an existing one. Graphic designers begin by determining the needs and preferences of clients and potential users, buyers, or viewers.

For example, if a graphic designer is working on a company logo, he or she will likely meet with company representatives to discuss such points as how and where the company is going to use the logo and what size, color, and shape preferences company executives might have. Project budgets must be respected: A design that may be perfect in every way but that is too costly to reproduce is basically useless. Graphic designers may need to compare their ideas with similar ones from other companies and analyze the image they project. They must have a good knowledge of how various colors, shapes, and layouts affect the viewer psychologically.

After a plan has been conceived and the details worked out, the graphic designer does some preliminary designs (generally two or three) to present to the client for approval. The client may reject the preliminary designs entirely and request a new one, or he or she may ask the designer to make alterations. The designer then goes back to the drawing board to attempt a new design or make the requested changes. This process continues until the client approves the design.

Once a design has been approved, the graphic designer prepares the piece for professional reproduction, or printing. The printer may require what is called a mechanical, in which the artwork and copy are arranged on a white board just as it is to be photographed, or the designer may be asked to submit an electronic copy of the design. Either way, designers must have a good understanding of the printing process, including color separation, paper properties, and half-tone (photograph) reproduction.

REQUIREMENTS

High School
While in high school, take any art and design courses that are available. Computer classes are also helpful, particularly those that teach page layout programs or art and photography manipulation programs. Working on the school newspaper or yearbook can provide valuable design experience. You could also volunteer to design flyers or posters for school events.

Postsecondary Training
A bachelor's degree in graphic design is generally required for entry-level positions. About 300 colleges and art schools offer art and graphic design programs that are accredited by the National Association of Schools of Art and Design. At many schools, graphic design students must take a year of basic art and design courses

before being accepted into the bachelor's degree program. In addition, applicants to the bachelor's degree programs in graphic arts may be asked to submit samples of their work to prove artistic ability. Many schools and employers depend on samples, or portfolios, to evaluate the applicants' skills in graphic design.

Many programs increasingly emphasize the importance of using computers for design work. Computer proficiency will be very important in the years to come. Interested individuals should select an academic program that incorporates computer training into the curriculum, or train themselves on their own.

A bachelor of fine arts program at a four-year college or university may include courses such as principles of design, art and art history, painting, sculpture, mechanical and architectural drawing, architecture, computer design, basic engineering, fashion designing and sketching, garment construction, and textiles. Such degrees are desirable but not always necessary for obtaining a position as a graphic designer.

Other Requirements

As with all artists, graphic designers need a degree of artistic talent, creativity, and imagination. They must be sensitive to beauty, have an eye for detail, and have a strong sense of color, balance, and proportion. Much of these qualities come naturally to potential graphic designers, but skills can be developed and improved through training, both on the job and in professional schools, colleges, and universities.

More and more graphic designers need solid computer skills and working knowledge of several of the common drawing, image editing, and page layout programs. Graphic design can be done on both Macintosh systems and on PCs; in fact, many designers have both types of computers in their studios.

With or without specialized education, graphic designers seeking employment should have a good portfolio containing samples of their best work. The graphic designer's portfolio is extremely important and can make a difference when an employer must choose between two otherwise equally qualified candidates.

A period of on-the-job training is expected for all beginning designers. The length of time it takes to become fully qualified as a graphic designer may run from one to three years, depending on prior education and experience, as well as innate talent.

EXPLORING

If you are interested in a career in graphic design, there are a number of ways to find out whether you have the talent, ambition, and perseverance to succeed in the field. Take as many art and design courses as possible while still in high school and become proficient using computers. To get an insider's view of various design occupations, you could enlist the help of art teachers or school counselors to make arrangements to tour design firms and interview designers.

While in school, seek out practical experience by participating in school and community projects that call for design talents. These might include such activities as building sets for plays, setting up exhibits, planning seasonal and holiday displays, and preparing programs and other printed materials. If you are interested in publication design, work on the school newspaper or yearbook is invaluable.

Part-time and summer jobs are excellent ways to become familiar with the day-to-day requirements of a design job and gain some basic related experience. Possible places of employment include design studios, design departments in advertising agencies and manufacturing companies, department and furniture stores, flower shops, workshops that produce ornamental items, and museums. Museums also use a number of volunteer workers. Inexperienced people are often employed as sales, clerical, or general assistants; those with a little more education and experience may qualify for jobs in which they have a chance to develop actual design skills and build portfolios of completed design projects.

EMPLOYERS

Graphic designers hold approximately 286,100 jobs. They work in many different industries, including the wholesale and retail trade (such as department stores, furniture and home furnishings stores, apparel stores, and florist shops); manufacturing industries (such as machinery, motor vehicles, aircraft, metal products, instruments, apparel, textiles, printing, and publishing); service industries (such as business services, engineering, and architecture); construction firms; and government agencies. Public relations and publicity firms, advertising agencies, and mail-order houses all have graphic design departments. The publishing industry is a primary employer of graphic designers, including book publishers, magazines, newspapers, and newsletters.

About 25 percent of all graphic designers are self-employed, a higher proportion than is found in most other occupations. These freelance designers sell their services to multiple clients.

STARTING OUT

The best way to enter the field of graphic design is to have a strong portfolio. Potential employers rely on portfolios to evaluate talent and how that talent might be used to fit the company's needs. Beginning graphic designers can assemble a portfolio from work completed at school, in art classes, and in part-time or freelance jobs. The portfolio should continually be updated to reflect the designer's growing skills so it will always be ready for possible job changes.

Those just starting out can apply directly to companies that employ designers. Many colleges and professional schools have placement services to help graduates find positions, and sometimes it is possible to get a referral from a previous part-time employer or volunteer coordinator.

ADVANCEMENT

As part of their on-the-job training, beginning graphic designers generally are given simpler tasks and work under direct supervision. As they gain experience, they move up to more complex work with increasingly less supervision. Experienced graphic designers, especially those with leadership capabilities, may be promoted to chief designer, design department head, or other supervisory positions.

Graphic designers with strong computer skills can move into other computer-related positions with additional education. Some may become interested in graphics programming in order to further improve their computer design capabilities. Others may want to become involved with multimedia and interactive technology. Video games, touch-screen displays in stores, and even laser light shows are all products of *multimedia graphic designers.*

When designers develop personal styles that are in high demand in the marketplace, they sometimes go into business for themselves. Freelance design work can be erratic, however, so usually only the most experienced designers with an established client base can count on consistent full-time work.

EARNINGS

The range of salaries for graphic designers is quite broad. Many earn as little as $20,000, while others make more than $100,000. Salaries depend primarily on the nature and scope of the employer. The U.S. Department of Labor reports that in 2008, graphic designers earned a median salary of $42,400; the highest paid 10 percent earned $74,660 or more, while the lowest paid 10 percent earned $26,110 or less. The American Institute of Graphic Arts/Aquent Salary Survey 2008 reports that designers earned a median salary of $45,000, while senior designers earned a median of $60,000 annually. Salaried designers who advance to the position of creative/design director earned a median of $90,000 a year.

Self-employed designers can earn a lot one year and substantially more or less the next. Their earnings depend on individual talent and business ability, but, in general, are higher than those of salaried designers. Although like any self-employed individual, freelance designers must pay their own insurance costs and taxes and are not compensated for vacation or sick days.

Graphic designers who work for large corporations receive full benefits, including health insurance, paid vacation, and sick leave.

WORK ENVIRONMENT

Most graphic designers work regular hours in clean, comfortable, pleasant offices or studios. Conditions vary depending on the design specialty. Some graphic designers work in small establishments with few employees; others work in large organizations with large design departments. Some deal mostly with their coworkers; others may have a lot of public contact. Freelance designers are paid by the assignment. To maintain a steady income, they must constantly strive to please their clients and to find new ones. At times, graphic designers may have to work long, irregular hours in order to complete an especially ambitious project.

OUTLOOK

Employment for qualified graphic designers is expected to grow about as fast as the average for all occupations through 2018; employment should be especially strong for those involved with advertising, computer graphics, multimedia, and animation. As computer graphic and Web-based technology continues to advance, there will be a need for well-trained computer graphic designers. Companies that have always used graphic designers will expect their designers to perform work on computers. Companies for which graphic design was once too time consuming or costly are now sprucing up company newsletters and magazines, among other things, requiring the skills of design professionals.

Because the design field appeals to many talented individuals, competition is expected to be strong in all areas. Beginners and designers with only average talent or without formal education and technical skills may encounter some difficulty in finding a job.

FOR MORE INFORMATION

For more information about careers in graphic design, contact
American Institute of Graphic Arts
164 Fifth Avenue

New York, NY 10010-5901
Tel: 212-807-1990
http://www.aiga.org

Visit the NASAD Web site for information on schools.
National Association of Schools of Art and Design (NASAD)
11250 Roger Bacon Drive, Suite 21
Reston, VA 20190-5248
Tel: 703-437-0700
E-mail: info@arts-accredit.org
http://nasad.arts-accredit.org

For information on careers in environmental design, contact
Society for Environmental Graphic Design
1000 Vermont Avenue, Suite 400
Washington, DC 20005-4921
Tel: 202-638-5555
http://www.segd.org

To read an online newsletter featuring competitions, examples of top designers' work, and industry news, visit the society's Web site.
Society of Publication Designers
27 Union Square West, Suite 207
New York, NY 10003-3305
Tel: 212-223-3332
E-mail: mail@spd.org
http://www.spd.org

INTERVIEW

Michael Cabonce is a graphic designer and the owner of Michael Cabonce Illustration and Design. He discussed his career with the editors of Careers in Focus: Design.

Q. Please tell us about your business. How long have you worked in the field?

A. I have been working in the field of illustration and design for more than 20 years. I have my own company—it's basically just me. I do illustration and design work for nonprofit, education, and business organizations. Most of the work involves publications such as newsletters, magazines, programs, or brochures. I also do some advertising, posters, and direct mail.

Q. Why did you decide to enter this field?

A. I have skills in drawing and painting, which led me to look for a career that used my skills. I decided to go into graphic design because I could see a defined career path and a way of making a living. I worked for an advertising agency after college and then for a hospital graphic/printing department. I've had my own studio for the past 10 years.

Q. What are the most important professional qualities for graphic designers?

A. You should be able to work well with others—your colleagues as well as your clients. Listening and networking are important. Skills in sales or marketing are valuable for your own business as well as for that of your clients. On top of being creative … there are a lot of skills needed for graphic designers/illustrators.

Q. What do you like most and least about your job?

A. I like getting paid. I don't like billing. I like meeting people. I don't like networking. But I still do my own billing and I still network.
   I like the process of design—generating ideas, coming up with concepts, doing research, exploring different ways of putting things together and then producing the actual art, making the ideas tangible and real.

Q. What advice would you give to high school students who are interested in becoming graphic designers?

A. Work on developing your graphic design skills and finding real work experience. If you have opportunities to do real design work, do it. Design the posters, advertising, programs, or Web pages for your school, local events, or your community. Do it like a professional would. Design on a computer and use professional media and materials.

Greeting Card Designers and Writers

OVERVIEW

Greeting card designers and writers either work as freelancers or as staff members of greeting card and gift manufacturers. Designers use artistic skills to create illustrated or photographic images for cards, posters, mugs, and other items generally sold in card shops and on the Internet; writers compose the expressions, poems, and jokes that accompany the images. The Greeting Card Association estimates that there are more than 3,000 large and small greeting card publishers in America.

HISTORY

The Valentine is considered by many to be the earliest form of greeting card. Up until the fifth century, Romans celebrated a fertility festival called Lupercalia every February 15. At the feast, women wrote love notes and dropped them in an urn; the men would pick a note from the urn, then seek the company of the woman who composed the note. But the mass-produced holiday cards we know today didn't originate until the 1880s in England and America. With printing costs and postage rates low, the colorful, cheerful, and beautifully illustrated cards of the day quickly grew in popularity.

Today, greeting cards are not only available in paper format, but are also sent electronically via e-mail. One thing that hasn't changed is that greeting cards

QUICK FACTS

School Subjects
Art
Computer science
English

Personal Skills
Artistic
Communication/ideas

Work Environment
Primarily indoors
Primarily one location

Minimum Education Level
Bachelor's degree

Salary Range
$26,110 to $42,400 to
$74,660+ (designers)
$28,020 to $53,070 to
$106,630+ (writers)

Certification or Licensing
None available

Outlook
About as fast as the average

DOT
142 (designers)
132 (writers)

GOE
01.04.02 (designers)
01.02.01 (writers)

NOC
5241 (designers)
5121 (writers)

O*NET-SOC
27-1024.00 (designers)
27-3043.05 (writers)

continue to be an extremely popular method of communicating with friends and family.

THE JOB

From sincere statements of love to jocular jabs, the contemporary greeting card industry provides a note for practically every expression. Hallmark and American Greetings are the biggest names in the business, offering traditional cards and electronic cards (known as e-cards) for many occasions. Other card companies have carved out their own individual niches—specializing in hand-drawn cards or cards that focus on a particular holiday or life event such as a breakup or wedding. Though some of these companies use the talents of full-time staff writers and designers, others rely on freelancers to submit ideas, images, and expressions. In addition to greeting card production, some companies buy words and images for e-mail greetings, and for lines of products like mugs, posters, pillows, and balloons.

Working from home offices, greeting card writers and designers come up with their ideas, then submit them to companies for consideration. Artists and photographers submit reproductions of their work, rather than their originals, because some companies don't

Facts About Greeting Cards

- Americans exchange 7 billion greeting cards annually.
- The average U.S. household purchases 30 greeting cards a year.
- Women buy 80 percent of greeting cards.
- Approximately 500 million e-cards are sent worldwide each year.
- There are more than 3,000 greeting card companies in the United States.
- Annual sales in the U.S. greeting card industry exceed $7.5 billion.
- Technological trends in the design and presentation of greeting cards include cards that feature lenticular design, which uses hologram-like technology to make cards appear to "move"; cards that feature sound chips, which allow them to feature music or audio snippets from pop culture; and "light cards," which feature LED lights to make them more exciting.

Source: Greeting Card Association

return unaccepted submissions or may lose the submissions in the review process. Artists submit prints, color copies, duplicate transparencies, PDFs, or CDs. Writers submit their ideas on index cards. Additionally, some companies accept submissions online.

Freelance greeting card designers and writers must also have good business and marketing skills. They need to keep track of assignments and payments and constantly seek out new clients in order to stay in business.

REQUIREMENTS

High School

Hone your writing and artistic skills in high school by taking English and art classes. Since many designers use computers to create their designs, computer science courses also will be helpful.

Postsecondary Training

A college education is not necessary for freelancing as an artist and writer; however, card companies looking to hire you for a full-time staff position typically require a bachelor's degree in English, creative writing, graphic design, or commercial arts. Even if you only want to freelance, community college courses that instruct you in the use of computer design programs can help you to create professional-looking images for submission to companies.

Certification or Licensing

No certification program exists for greeting card writers or designers. However, if you decide to print your own cards and sell them to stores and representatives, you may be required by your state to maintain a business license.

Other Requirements

Greeting card writers and designers should be patient, persistent, and capable of accepting rejection. They should also be highly creative and have a good sense of humor. The industry is very competitive, and writers and designers must create work that catches the attention of their employer and, ultimately, customers. Self-employed writers and designers must be self-motivated and be committed to working extremely hard to meet deadlines and attract new clients.

EXPLORING

Try writing and designing your own greeting cards. There are many software programs that will help you create attractive cards, stationery, and newsletters. Ask your high school English teacher or counselor to set up an interview with a greeting card designer or freelance writer.

EMPLOYERS

As a freelancer, you can work anywhere in the country and submit your work through the mail. *Artist's & Graphic Designer's Market* and *Writer's Market,* reference books published annually by Writer's Digest Books (http://www.writersdigest.com), include sections listing the greeting card companies that accept submissions from freelance artists and writers. While some companies only buy a few ideas a year, others buy hundreds of ideas. Hallmark, by far the largest greeting card manufacturer, doesn't accept unsolicited ideas, but hires many creative people for full-time staff positions. However, because of Hallmark's reputation as a great employer, competition for those positions is high.

STARTING OUT

Get to know the market by visiting local card shops; find out what's popular, and what kinds of cards each company sells. Visit the Web sites of the greeting card companies listed in *Artist's & Graphic Designer's Market* and *Writer's Market* and study their online catalogs. Most companies have very specific guidelines; one may publish only humorous cards, while another may only publish inspirational poems. Once you have a good sense of what companies are looking for, contact manufacturers, find out their submission guidelines, and submit samples of your work.

Another opportunity to break into the industry is through an internship. Every year, Hallmark holds a competition for its creative internships. (See its contact information at the end of this article.)

ADVANCEMENT

After you've submitted a lot of your work to many different companies, you'll begin to make connections with people in the business. These connections can be valuable, leading you to jobs with better pay (such as royalties and percentages) and exclusive contracts. As you get to know the business better, you may choose to produce and market your own line of cards. If you work full time for a company, you might advance to the position of lead designer or manager of a design department.

EARNINGS

Salaries vary widely among freelance greeting card writers and designers. Some card designers and writers sell only a few ideas a year. Others make a great deal of money, working exclusively with a company, or by manufacturing and distributing their own lines of cards and products. Card companies typically pay freelancers fees for each idea they buy. Some manufacturers may offer a royalty payment plan, including an initial advance. A small company may pay as little as $15 for an idea, while a larger company may pay $150 or more.

According to the U.S. Department of Labor, graphic designers earned a median annual salary of $42,400 in 2008, but pay ranged from less than $26,110 to more than $74,660. Salaried writers of all types earned a median salary of $53,070 in 2008. The lowest 10 percent earned less than $28,020 while the highest paid writers earned more than $106,630 a year.

Greeting card designers and writers who work for a company usually receive benefits such as vacation days, sick leave, health and life insurance, and a savings and pension program. Self-employed designers and editors must provide their own benefits.

WORK ENVIRONMENT

Both writers and designers spend most of their time in an office, whether at home or in a company's space. Much of their work is done on a computer, whether they are designing images or writing copy. However, coming up with the initial ideas may involve a more creative routine. Many artists have certain activities that inspire them, such as listening to music, looking at photography and art books, or reading a novel.

OUTLOOK

According to the Greeting Card Association (GCA), the greeting card industry's retail sales have increased steadily from $2.1 billion in 1980 to more than $7.5 billion today. From designing animated e-mail messages to greeting card software programs, greeting card writers and designers will likely find more and more outlets for their work. Advances in Web technology should also aid the card designer in posting his or her ideas and images online to invite companies to browse, download, and purchase ideas.

Average growth is expected for this career in coming years. Despite the growing popularity of e-mail, e-cards, and other communications technology, the GCA says the industry will not be adversely affected. E-cards are not as personal as standard greeting cards, nor are they appropriate for many situations, such as weddings, anniversaries, or for expressing sympathy. "Although e-mail, text messaging and phone calls are valued by Americans for helping them communicate with family and friends, the majority of Americans say they prefer the old-fashioned handwritten card or letter to make someone feel truly special," the GCA says.

FOR MORE INFORMATION

For information on the industry and artist and writer guidelines, check out the following Web site:
Greeting Card Association
750 National Press Building
529 14th Street, NW
Washington, DC 20045-1000
Tel: 202-393-1778
E-mail: info@greetingcard.org
http://www.greetingcard.org

For information on Hallmark's internship program and career opportunities, visit
Hallmark Cards Inc.
Customer Service
P.O. Box 419034
Mail Drop 216
Kansas City, MO 64141-9034
Tel: 800-425-5627
http://www.hallmark.com

Industrial Designers

OVERVIEW

Industrial designers combine technical knowledge of materials, machines, and production with artistic talent to improve the appearance and function of machine-made products. There are approximately 44,300 commercial and industrial designers employed in the United States.

HISTORY

Although industrial design as a separate and unique profession did not develop in the United States until the 1920s, it has its origins in colonial America and the industrial revolution. When colonists were faced with having to make their own products rather than relying on imported goods, they learned to modify existing objects and create new ones. As the advent of the industrial revolution drew near, interest in machinery and industry increased.

One of the earliest examples of industrial design is found in Eli Whitney's production of muskets. In 1800, he promised to manufacture several thousand muskets for the government using the principles of standardization and interchangeable parts. Designs and manufacturing processes for each musket part had to be created. This early example of industrial design involved not only designing an individual product but also the manufacturing processes and the production equipment.

The industrial revolution brought about the mass production of objects and increased machine manufacturing. As production capabilities grew, a group of entrepreneurs, inventors, and designers emerged. Together, these individuals determined products that could be mass-produced and figured out ways to manufacture them.

QUICK FACTS

School Subjects
Art
Mathematics

Personal Skills
Artistic
Technical/scientific

Work Environment
Primarily indoors
Primarily one location

Minimum Education Level
Bachelor's degree

Salary Range
$31,400 to $57,350 to
$125,000

Certification or Licensing
None available

Outlook
About as fast as the average

DOT
142

GOE
01.04.02

NOC
2252

O*NET-SOC
27-1021.00

In the early 1900s, the number of products available to the public grew, as did the purchasing power of individuals. Manufacturers realized that in order to compete with imported goods and skilled craftspersons, they needed to offer a wide variety of products that were well designed and affordable. At that time, manufactured products were designed to be functional, utilitarian, and easily produced by machines. Little attention was paid to aesthetics. Product designs were copied from imported items, and there was little original design.

Consumers were growing increasingly dissatisfied with the products they were offered. They felt that machine-made goods were, in many cases, ugly and unattractive. Manufacturers did not initially respond to these complaints. For example, Henry Ford continued to manufacture only one style of car, the Model T, despite criticism that it looked like a tin can. Ford was unconcerned because he sold more cars than anyone else. When General Motors started selling its attractive Chevrolet in 1926, and it outsold the Ford Model T, Ford finally recognized the importance of styling and design.

Advertising convincingly demonstrated the importance of design. Those products with artistic features sold better, and manufacturers realized that design did play an important role both in marketing and manufacturing. By 1927, manufacturers were hiring people solely to advise them on design features. Industrial design came to represent a new profession: the practice of using aesthetic design features to create manufactured goods that were economical, served a specific purpose, and satisfied the psychological needs of consumers. Most of the early industrial designers came from Europe until design schools were established in America.

Industrial design as a profession grew rapidly in the years from 1927 until World War II. Many of the early industrial designers established their own firms rather than working directly for a manufacturer. After the war, consumer goods proliferated, which helped the field continue to grow. Manufacturers paid more attention to style and design in an effort to make their products stand out in the marketplace. They began to hire in-house designers. Today, industrial designers play a significant role in both designing new products and determining which products may be successful in the marketplace.

THE JOB

Industrial designers are an integral part of the manufacturing process. They work on creating designs for new products and redesigning existing products. Before a product can be manufactured, a design must be created that specifies its form, function, and appearance. Industrial designers must pay attention to the purpose of the proposed product, anticipated use by consumers, economic factors affecting its design and manufacture, and material and safety requirements.

Industrial designers are usually part of a team that includes engineers, marketing specialists, production personnel, sales representatives, and sometimes, top manufacturing managers. Before the design process actually begins, market research or surveys may be conducted that analyze how well a product is performing, what its market share is, and how well competitors' products are doing. Also, feasibility studies may be conducted to determine whether an existing design should be changed or a new product created to keep or gain market share.

Once a determination is made to create a new design, an industrial designer is assigned to the project. The designer reviews study results and meets with other design team members to develop a concept. The designer studies the features of the proposed product as well as the material requirements and manufacturing costs and requirements. Several designs are sketched and other team members are consulted.

Some designers still create sketches by hand, but most use design software that allows them to create sketches on a computer. Once a preliminary design is selected, designers work out all of the details. They calculate all of the measurements of each part of the design, identify specific components, select necessary materials, and choose colors and other visual elements. A detailed design is then submitted to engineers and other design team members for review.

In some cases, a model or prototype may be built; however, computer-aided design programs now allow engineers to test design features before this stage. Engineers test for performance, strength, durability, and other factors to ensure that a product actually performs as planned and meets all safety and industrial standards. If any part of a product fails to meet test standards, the design is sent back to the industrial designer for revisions.

This process continues until the design passes all test stages. At this point, a model may be built of clay, foam, wood, or other materials to serve as a guide for production. In some cases, a prototype made of the actual materials and components will be built. The design, along with all computer data and any models and prototypes, is turned over to the production department, which is then responsible for manufacturing it.

Industrial designers may also become involved in the marketing and advertising promotion of products. They may name the new product, design the product's packaging, plan promotional

An industrial designer at Microsoft holds the final version of the Microsoft Natural Wireless Laser Mouse 6000. Models used in its design are on the designer's desk. *(Ted S. Warren, AP Photo)*

campaigns or advertising strategies, and create artwork used for advertising.

Industrial designers may design the layout of franchised businesses, such as clothing stores or gas stations, so that they present a coordinated company image. This type of design can also include developing company symbols, trademarks, and logos.

Designers may work for a design firm or directly for a manufacturing company. They may freelance or set up their own consulting firms. Corporate designers may be part of a large team with designers at various locations. Computer networking allows several designers to work simultaneously on the same project. Using this approach, a designer creates one part of a design, for example, the electronic components, while another designer creates another part, such as the mechanical housing. A variation on the multidesigner approach schedules designers on different shifts to work on the same project.

Technology is changing the way industrial designers work. Computer-aided industrial design tools are revolutionizing the way products are designed and manufactured. These programs allow designers and engineers to test products during the design stage so that design flaws are identified before prototypes are built. Other programs allow product models to be tested online. Designs can be sent directly to machine tools that produce 3-D models. All of these advances decrease the time necessary to design a product, test it, and manufacture it.

REQUIREMENTS

High School
In high school, take as many art and computer classes as possible in addition to college preparatory classes in English, social studies, algebra, geometry, and science. Classes in mechanical drawing may be helpful, but drafting skills are being replaced by the ability to use computers to create graphics and manipulate objects. Science

Useful Publications for Industrial Designers

- *Abitare* (http://www.abitare.it/langswitch_lang/en)
- *Car Styling* (http://www.carstylingmag.com)
- *Contract* (http://www.contractdesign.com)
- *Design News* (http://www.designnews.com)
- *HOW* (http://www.howdesign.com)
- *I.D. Magazine* (http://www.id-mag.com)
- *Machine Design* (http://machinedesign.com)
- *Medical Device & Diagnostic Industry* (http://www.devicelink.com/mddi)
- *Metropolis* (http://www.metropolismag.com/cda)
- *Playthings* (http://www.playthings.com)
- *Visual Merchandising & Store Design* (http://vmsd.com)

classes, such as physics and chemistry, are also becoming more important as industrial designers select materials and components for products and need to have a basic understanding of scientific principles. Shop classes, such as machine shop, metalworking, and woodworking, are also useful and provide training in using hand and machine tools.

Postsecondary Training
A bachelor's degree in fine arts or industrial design is recommended, although some employers accept diplomas from art schools. Training is offered through art schools, art departments of colleges and universities, and technical colleges. Most bachelor's degree programs require four or five years to complete. Some schools also offer a master's degree, which requires two years of additional study. Often, art schools grant a diploma for three years of study in industrial design. Bachelor's degree programs in industrial design are offered by approximately 40 schools accredited by the National Association of Schools of Art and Design.

School programs vary; some emphasize engineering and technical work, while others emphasize art background. Certain basic courses are common to every school: 2-D design (color theory, spatial organization) and 3-D design (abstract sculpture, art structures). Students also have a great deal of studio practice, learning to make models of clay, plaster, wood, and other easily worked materials. Some schools even use metalworking machinery. Technically oriented schools generally require a course in basic engineering. Schools offering degree programs also require courses in English, history, science, and other basic subjects. Such courses as merchandising and business are important for anyone working in a field so closely connected with the consumer. Most schools also offer classes in computer-aided design and computer graphics. One of the most essential skills for success as an industrial designer is the ability to use design software.

Other Requirements
Industrial designers are creative, have artistic ability, and are able to work closely with others in a collaborative style. In general, designers do not crave fame or recognition because designing is a joint project involving the skills of many people. In most cases, industrial designers remain anonymous and behind the scenes. Successful designers can accept criticism and differences of opinion and be open to new ideas.

EXPLORING

An excellent way to uncover an aptitude for design and to gain practical experience in using computers is to take a computer graphics course through an art school, high school continuing education program, technical school, or community college. Some community colleges allow high school students to enroll in classes if no comparable course is offered at the high school level. If no formal training is available, teach yourself how to use a popular graphics software package.

Summer or part-time employment in an industrial design office is a good way to learn more about the profession and what industrial designers do. Another option is to work in an advertising agency or for a market research firm. Although these companies most likely won't have an industrial designer on staff, they will provide exposure to how to study consumer trends and plan marketing promotions.

Pursue hobbies such as sculpting, ceramics, jewelry making, woodworking, and sketching to develop creative and artistic abilities. Reading about industrial design can also be very beneficial. Publications such as *Design News* (http://www.designnews.com) contain many interesting and informative articles that describe different design products and report on current trends. This magazine can be found at many public libraries. Read books on the history of industrial design to learn about interesting case studies on the development of specific products.

EMPLOYERS

Approximately 44,300 commerical and industrial designers are employed in the United States. Industrial designers work in all areas of industry. Some specialize in consumer products, such as household appliances, home entertainment items, personal computers, clothing, jewelry, and car stereos. Others work in designing automobiles, electronic devices, airplanes, biomedical products, medical equipment, measuring instruments, or office equipment. Most designers specialize in a specific area of manufacturing and work on only a few types of products.

STARTING OUT

Most employers prefer to hire someone who has a degree or diploma from a college, art school, or technical school. Persons with engineering, architectural, or other scientific backgrounds also have a good chance at entry-level jobs, especially if they have artistic and creative talent. When interviewing for a job, a designer should be prepared to present a portfolio of work.

Job openings may be listed through a college career services office or in classified ads in newspapers or trade magazines. Qualified beginners may also apply directly to companies that hire industrial designers. Several directories listing industrial design firms can be found in most public libraries. In addition, lists of industrial design firms appear periodically in magazines such as *BusinessWeek* and *Engineering News-Record*. Also, a new industrial designer can read *Getting an Industrial Design Job* at the Industrial Designers Society of America's Web site, http://www.idsa.org.

ADVANCEMENT

Entry-level industrial designers usually begin as assistants to other designers. They do routine work and hold little responsibility for design changes. With experience and the necessary qualifications, the designer may be promoted to a higher-ranking position with major responsibility for design. Experienced designers may be promoted to project managers or move into supervisory positions. Supervisory positions may include overseeing and coordinating the work of several designers, including freelancers and industrial designers at outside agencies. Some senior designers are given a free hand in designing products. With experience, established reputation, and financial backing, some industrial designers decide to open their own consulting firms.

EARNINGS

According to the Industrial Designers Society of America, the average starting salary for industrial designers is $36,000. Designers with five years' experience earn an average of $58,000 a year. Senior designers with 10 years' experience earn $73,000. Industrial designers with 19 years or more experience earn average salaries of $125,000. Managers who direct design departments in large companies earn substantially more. Owners or partners of consulting firms have fluctuating incomes, depending on their business for the year.

According to the U.S. Department of Labor, industrial designers earned a median annual salary of $57,350 in 2008. The lowest paid 10 percent earned less than $31,400 annually, and the top paid 10 percent earned more than $97,770.

Industrial designers usually receive paid vacations and holidays, sick leave, hospitalization and insurance benefits, and pension programs.

WORK ENVIRONMENT

Industrial designers enjoy generally pleasant work conditions. In many companies, the atmosphere is relaxed and casual. Most designers spend a significant amount of time at either a computer workstation or drawing board. Most industrial designers work at least 40 hours a week, with overtime frequently required. There is a lot of pressure to speed up the design/development process and get products to market as soon as possible. For some designers, this can mean regularly working 10 to 20 hours or more of overtime a week. Working on weekends and into the evening can be required to run a special computer program or to work on a project with a tight deadline. Designers who freelance, or work for themselves, set their own hours but may work more than 40 hours a week in order to meet the needs of their clients.

OUTLOOK

Employment of industrial designers is expected to grow about as fast as the average for all occupations through 2018, according to the U.S. Department of Labor (DOL). This favorable outlook is based on the need to improve product quality and safety, to design new products for the global marketplace, and to design high-technology products in consumer electronics, medicine, and transportation. The DOL predicts that designers who combine business expertise with an educational background in engineering and computer-aided design will have the best employment prospects.

Despite the demand for industrial designers, many companies prefer to outsource a significant amount of their work. This is a growing trend within the industry that may make it more difficult for a beginning worker to find an entry-level job. In addition, this is a profession that is somewhat controlled by the economic climate. It thrives in times of prosperity and declines in periods of recession.

FOR MORE INFORMATION

For information on opportunities for women in industrial design, contact

Association of Women Industrial Designers
Old Chelsea Station
PO Box 468
New York, NY 10008-0461
E-mail: info@awidweb.com
http://www.awidweb.com

For information on careers, educational programs, and a free copy of Getting an Industrial Design Job, *contact*
Industrial Designers Society of America
45195 Business Court, Suite 250
Dulles, VA 20166-6717
Tel: 703-707-6000
http://www.idsa.org

For information on accredited design schools, contact
National Association of Schools of Art and Design
11250 Roger Bacon Drive, Suite 21
Reston, VA 20190-5248
Tel: 703-437-0700
E-mail: info@arts-accredit.org
http://nasad.arts-accredit.org

Interior Designers and Decorators

OVERVIEW

Interior designers and *interior decorators* evaluate, plan, and design the interior areas of residential, commercial, and industrial structures. In addition to helping clients select equipment and fixtures, they supervise the coordination of colors and materials, obtain estimates and costs within the client's budget, and oversee the execution and installation of the project. They also often advise clients on architectural requirements, space planning, and the function and purpose of the environment.

There are approximately 71,700 interior designers working in the United States. They are employed by interior design or architectural firms, department stores, furniture stores, hotel chains, and large corporations.

HISTORY

Appreciation for beauty has been expressed in many artforms, including music, painting, sculpture, and poetry. One way to make such beauty a part of everyday life is through decoration of the interiors of buildings. Individuals throughout history have added personal touches of decoration to their homes. Until recently, however, major design and decorating projects have been the privilege of the wealthy.

Artists such as Michelangelo were employed to design and beautify palaces and other buildings, making use of sculpture, paintings, and other wall coverings. Kings sometimes made names for themselves by the decorating trends initiated in their palaces. Such trends came to include furniture, draperies, and often clothing. Home designs and furniture were either largely functional, as in the early American tradition, or extremely ornate, as in the style of Louis XIV of France.

As our society prospered, the field of interior design emerged. While Elsie de Wolfe was the first person to actually practice interior design as a separate profession in 1905, it wasn't until the 1950s that the design revolution really began. Today, design professionals plan interiors of homes, restaurants, hotels, hospitals, theaters, stores, offices, and other buildings.

THE JOB

The terms *interior designer* and *interior decorator* are sometimes used interchangeably. However, there is an important distinction between the two. Interior designers plan and create the overall design for interior spaces, while interior decorators focus on the decorative aspects of the design and furnishing of interiors. A further distinction concerns the type of interior space on which the design or decorating professional works. Specifically, *residential designers* focus on individual homes, while *contract* or *commercial designers* specialize in office buildings, industrial complexes, hotels, hospitals, restaurants, schools, factories, and other nonresidential environments.

Interior designers and decorators perform a wide variety of services, depending on the type of project and the clients' requirements. A job may range from designing and decorating a single room in a private residence to coordinating the entire interior arrangement of a huge building complex. In addition to planning the interiors of new buildings, interior professionals also redesign existing interiors.

Design and decorating specialists begin by evaluating a project. They first consider how the space will be used. In addition to suiting the project's functional requirements, designs must address the needs, desires, tastes, and budget of the client as well. The designer often works closely with the architect in planning the complete layout of rooms and use of space. The designer's plans must work well with the architect's blueprints and comply with other building requirements. Design work of this kind is usually done in connection with the building or renovation of large structures.

Interior professionals may design the furniture and accessories to be used on a project, or they might work with materials that are already available. They select and plan the arrangement of furniture, draperies, floor coverings, wallpaper, paint, and other decorations. They make their decisions only after considering general style, scale of furnishings, colors, patterns, flow, lighting, safety, communication, and a host of other factors. They must also be familiar with local, state, and federal laws as well as building codes and other related regulations.

Although interior designers and decorators may consult with clients throughout the conceptual phase of the design project, they usually make a formal presentation once the design has been formulated. Such presentations may include sketches, scaled floor plans, drawings, models, color charts, photographs of furnishings, and samples of materials for upholstery, draperies, and wall coverings. Designers and decorators also usually provide a cost estimate of furnishings, materials, labor, transportation, and incidentals required to complete the project.

Once plans have been approved by the client, the interior designer or decorator assembles materials—drapery fabrics, upholstery fabrics, new furniture, paint, and wallpaper—and supervises the work, often acting as agent for the client in contracting the services of craft workers and specifying custom-made merchandise. Interior professionals must be familiar with many materials used in furnishing. They must know when certain materials are suitable, how they will blend with other materials, and how they will wear. They must also be familiar with historical periods influencing design and have a knack for using and combining the best contributions of these designs of the past. Since designers and decorators supervise the work done from their plans, they should know something about painting, carpet laying, carpentry, cabinet making, and other craft areas. In addition, they must be able to buy materials and services at reasonable prices while producing quality work.

Some designers and decorators specialize in a particular aspect of interior design, such as furniture, carpeting, or artwork. Others concentrate on particular environments, such as offices, hospitals, restaurants, or transportation, including ships, aircraft, and trains. Still others specialize in the renovation of old buildings. In addition to researching the styles in which rooms were originally decorated and furnished, these workers often supervise the manufacture of furniture and accessories to be used.

Considerable paperwork is involved in interior design and decoration, much of it related to budgets and costs. Interior professionals must determine quantities and make and obtain cost estimates. In addition, designers and decorators write up and administer contracts, obtain permits, place orders, and check deliveries carefully. All of this work requires an ability to attend to detail in the business aspect of interior design.

REQUIREMENTS

High School

Although formal training is not always necessary in the field of interior design, it is becoming increasingly important and is usually essential for advancement. Most architectural firms, department stores, and design firms accept only professionally trained people, even for beginning positions.

If you're considering a career as an interior designer or decorator, classes in home economics, art history, design, fine arts, and drafting will prove to be valuable. Since interior design is both an art and a business, such courses as marketing, advertising, accounting, management, and general business are important as well.

Postsecondary Training

Professional schools offer two- or three-year certificate or diploma programs in interior design. Colleges and universities award undergraduate degrees in four-year programs, and graduate study is also available. The Council for Interior Design Accreditation (CIDA) accredits bachelor's degree programs in interior design. There are more than 150 accredited interior design programs offered through art, architecture, and home economics schools in the United States. The National Association of Schools of Art and Design also accredits colleges and universities with programs in art and design. College students interested in entering the interior design field should take courses in art history, architectural drawing and drafting, fine arts, furniture design, codes and standards of design, and computer-aided design, as well as classes that focus on the types of materials primarily used, such as fibers, wood, metals, and plastics. Knowledge of lighting and electrical equipment as well as furnishings, art pieces, and antiques, is important.

In addition to art and industry-specific areas of study, courses in business and management are vital to aspiring interior designers and decorators. Learning research methods will help you stay abreast of government regulations and safety standards. You should also have some knowledge of zoning laws, building codes, and other restrictions. Finally, keeping up with product performance and new developments in materials and manufacture is an important part of the ongoing education of the interior designer and decorator.

Art historians, people with architecture or environmental planning experience, and others with qualifications in commercial or industrial design may also qualify for employment in interior design.

Certification or Licensing

Currently, 29 states, the District of Columbia, and Puerto Rico require licensing for interior designers, according to the National Council for Interior Design Qualification (NCIDQ). Each of these states has its own requirements for licensing and regulations for practice, so it's important to contact the specific state in order to find out how one can apply. To become eligible for registration or licensing in these jurisdictions, applicants must satisfy experience and education requirements and take the National Council for Interior Design Qualification Examination.

To prepare students for this examination, the NCIDQ offers the Interior Design Experience Program. Program participants are required to complete 3,520 hours of documented experience in the following categories: Programming, Schematic Design, Design Development, Contract Documents, Contract Administration, and Professional Practice. According to the council, this experience may be achieved through "working directly in a competency area, by observing others who are engaged in such work, or by attending lectures, seminars, and continuing education courses." Students who have completed at least 96 semester credits hours (or 144 quarter credits hours of education) in a CIDA-accredited interior design program are eligible to participate.

Additionally, the National Kitchen and Bath Association offers several certifications to designers who specialize in kitchen and bath design.

Other Requirements

First and foremost, interior designers and decorators need to have artistic talent, including an eye for color, proportion, balance, and detail, and have the ability to visualize. Designers must be able to render an image clearly and carry it out consistently. At the same time, artistic taste and knowledge of current and enduring fashion trends are essential.

In addition, interior designers need to be able to supervise craft workers and work well with a variety of other people, including clients and suppliers. Designers should be creative, analytical, and ethical. They also need to be able to focus on the needs of clients, develop a global view, and have an appreciation of diversity. Finally, precision, patience, perseverance, enthusiasm, and attention to detail are vital.

EXPLORING

If you're thinking about becoming an interior designer or decorator, there are several ways to learn about the field. Visit Web sites such as Careers in Interior Design (http://www.careersininteriordesign.com), which provides an excellent overview of educational requirements and career paths in the field.

Courses in home economics or any of the fine arts, offered either at school or through a local organization, can give you a taste of some of the areas of knowledge needed by interior designers.

To get a sense of the actual work done by design specialists, you may be able to find a part-time or summer job in a department or furniture store. Such experience will enable you to learn more about the materials used in interior design and decorating and to see the store's interior design service in action. Since the business aspects of interior design are just as important as the creative side, any kind of general sales or business experience will prove to be valuable. As a salesperson at any type of store, for example, you'll learn how to talk to customers, write up orders, close sales, and much more.

In addition to learning about interior design itself, knowledge of auxiliary and support industries will be useful as well. To get a first-hand look at associated fields, you may want to arrange a visit to a construction site, examine an architect's blueprints, talk to someone who specializes in lighting, or tour a furniture manufacturing plant.

Ultimately, the best way to learn about interior design or decorating is to talk to a design professional. While interviewing an interior designer or decorator will be interesting and enlightening, finding a mentor who is doing the type of work that you may want to do in the future is ideal. Such a person can suggest other activities that may be of interest to you as you investigate the interior design field, provide you with the names of trade magazines and/or books that can shed some light on the industry, and serve as a resource for questions you might have.

EMPLOYERS

Approximately 71,700 interior designers and decorators are employed in the United States. Interior designers and decorators can be found wherever there is a need to style or beautify the interior environment of a building. The main professional areas in which they work are residential, government, commercial, retail, hospitality, education and research, health care, and facilities management.

In addition to "traditional" interior design and decorating opportunities, some professionals design theater, film, and television settings. A few designers become teachers, lecturers, or consultants, while others work in advertising and journalism.

The majority of interior designers and decorators work either for themselves or for companies employing fewer than five people.

Since the industry is not dominated by giant conglomerates or even mid-sized firms, employment opportunities are available all across the United States, as well as abroad, in cities both large and small.

STARTING OUT

Most large department stores and design firms with established reputations hire only trained interior designers and decorators. More often than not, these employers look for prospective employees with a good portfolio and a bachelor of fine arts degree. Many schools, however, offer apprenticeship or internship programs in cooperation with professional studios or offices of interior design. These programs make it possible for students to apply their academic training in an actual work environment prior to graduation.

After graduating from a two- or three-year training program (or a four-year university), the beginning interior professional must be prepared to spend one to three years as an assistant to an experienced designer or decorator before achieving full professional status. This is the usual method of entering the field of interior design and gaining membership in a professional organization.

Finding work as an assistant can often be difficult, so be prepared to take any related job. Becoming a sales clerk for interior furnishings, a shopper for accessories or fabrics, or even a receptionist or stockroom assistant can help you get a foot in the door and provide valuable experience as well.

ADVANCEMENT

While advancement possibilities are available, competition for jobs is intense and interior designers and decorators must possess a combination of talent, personality, and business sense to reach the top. Someone just starting out in the field must take a long-range career view, accept jobs that offer practical experience, and put up with long hours and occasionally difficult clients. It usually takes three to six years of practical, on-the-job experience in order to become a fully qualified interior designer or decorator.

As interior professionals gain experience, they can move into positions of greater responsibility and may eventually be promoted to such jobs as design department head or interior furnishings coordinator. Professionals who work with furnishings in architectural firms often become more involved in product design and sales. Designers and decorators can also establish their own businesses. Consulting is another common area of work for the established interior professional.

EARNINGS

Interior designers earned median annual salaries of $44,950 in 2008, according to the U.S. Department of Labor. The highest paid 10 percent earned more than $82,750, while the lowest paid 10 percent earned less than $27,230 annually. The U.S. Department of Labor reports the following mean salaries for interior designers by specialty: architectural and engineering services, $53,420; specialized design services, $52,490; and furniture stores, $46,170. In general, interior designers and decorators working in large urban areas make significantly more than those working in smaller cities.

Designers and decorators at interior design firms can earn a straight salary, a salary plus a bonus or commission, or a straight commission. Such firms sometimes pay their employees a percentage of the profits as well. Self-employed professionals may charge an hourly fee, a flat fee, or a combination of the two depending on the project. Some designers and decorators charge a percentage on the cost of materials bought for each project.

The benefits enjoyed by interior designers and decorators, like salaries and bonuses, depend on the particular employer. Benefits may include paid vacations, health and life insurance, paid sick or personal days, employee-sponsored retirement plans, and an employer-sponsored 401(k) program.

WORK ENVIRONMENT

Working conditions for interior designers and decorators vary, depending on where they are employed. While professionals usually have an office or a studio, they may spend the day at a department store, architecture firm, or construction site working with the decorating materials sold by the firm and the clients who have purchased them. In addition, designers often go on-site to consult with and supervise the projects being completed by various craft workers.

Whether designers or decorators are employed by a firm or operate their own businesses, much of their time is spent in clients' homes and businesses. While more and more offices are using the services of interior designers and decorators, the larger part of the business still lies in the area of home design. Residential designers and decorators work intimately with customers, planning, selecting materials, receiving instructions, and sometimes subtly guiding the customers' tastes and choices in order to achieve an atmosphere that is both aesthetic and functional.

While designers and decorators employed by department stores, furniture stores, or design firms often work regular 40-hour weeks, self-employed professionals usually work irregular hours—including evenings and weekends—in order to accommodate their clients' schedules. Deadlines must be met, and if there have been problems and delays on the job, the designer or decorator must work hard to complete the project on schedule. In general, the more successful the individual becomes, the longer and more irregular the hours.

The interior professional's main objective is ultimately to please the customer and thus establish a good reputation. Customers may be difficult at times. They may often change their minds, forcing the designer or decorator to revise plans. Despite difficult clients, the work is interesting and provides a variety of activities.

OUTLOOK

Employment opportunities are expected to be very good for interior designers and decorators through 2018, according to the U.S. Department of Labor. However, since the services of design professionals are in many ways a luxury, the job outlook is heavily dependent on the economy. In times of prosperity, there is a steady increase in jobs. When the economy slows down, however, opportunities in the field decrease markedly.

Marketing futurist Faith Popcorn predicts that people will be staying home more (cocooning) and that there will be an increase in what she calls "fantasy adventure." This trend is based on people's desire to stay at home but, at the same time, feel like they are in exotic, remote places. In the future, Popcorn sees homes containing rooms designed like Las Vegas-style resorts, African plains, and other interesting destinations. Both cocooning and fantasy adventure will further add to the many opportunities that will be available to interior designers.

According to the International Interior Design Association's Industry Advisory Council (IAC), a number of trends specific to the industry will also positively influence the employment outlook for interior designers and decorators. Clients in all market areas, for example, will develop an appreciation for the value of interior design work as well as increased respect for the interior professional's expertise. In addition, businesses, ever mindful of their employees' safety, health, and general welfare, will rely more heavily on designers to create interior atmospheres that will positively impact workplace performance.

The IAC also notes the importance of technology in the field of interior design. In addition to affecting the design of homes, technology will impact the production of design materials as well as create the need for multidisciplinary design. Professionals both familiar and comfortable with technology will definitely have an edge in an ever-competitive job market.

While competition for good designing and decorating positions is expected to be fierce, especially for those lacking experience, there is currently a great need for industrial interior designers in housing developments, offices, restaurants, hospital complexes, senior care facilities, hotels, and other large building projects. In addition, as construction of houses increases, there will be many projects available for residential designers and decorators. Designers with strong knowledge of ergonomics and green design will also enjoy excellent job prospects. Those who specialize in one aspect of interior design, such as kitchen or bath design, may have better employment prospects in this highly competitive field.

FOR MORE INFORMATION

For industry trends, career guidance, and other resources, contact
American Society of Interior Designers
608 Massachusetts Avenue, NE
Washington, DC 20002-6006
Tel: 202-546-3480
http://www.asid.org

For career information, visit
Careers in Interior Design
http://www.careersininteriordesign.com

For a list of accredited interior design programs, contact
Council for Interior Design Accreditation
206 Grandville Avenue, Suite 350
Grand Rapids, MI 49503-4014
Tel: 616-458-0400
E-mail: info@accredit-id.org
http://www.accredit-id.org

For information on continuing education, publications, and a list of accredited graduate programs in interior design, contact
Interior Design Educators Council
9100 Purdue Road, Suite 200
Indianapolis, IN 46268-3165
Tel: 317-328-4437
E-mail: info@idec.org
http://www.idec.org

For information on the industry, contact
International Interior Design Association
222 Merchandise Mart, Suite 567
Chicago, IL 60654-1103
Tel: 888-799-4432
E-mail: iidahq@iida.org
http://www.iida.com

For information on accredited interior design programs, contact
National Association of Schools of Art and Design
11250 Roger Bacon Drive, Suite 21
Reston, VA 20190-5248
Tel: 703-437-0700
E-mail: info@arts-accredit.org
http://nasad.arts-accredit.org

For information on the Interior Design Experience Program, contact
National Council for Interior Design Qualification
1602 L Street NW, Suite 200
Washington, DC 20036-5681
Tel: 202-721-0220
http://www.ncidq.org

For information on certification, contact
National Kitchen and Bath Association
687 Willow Grove Street
Hackettstown, NJ 07840-1713
Tel: 800-843-6522
http://www.nkba.org

INTERVIEW

Jane Irvine is the owner of Jane Irvine Interior Design. She has worked as an interior designer since 1987. (Visit http://www.jane irvineinteriordesign.com to learn more about her work.) Jane discussed her career with the editors of Careers in Focus: Design.

Q. Can you please tell us about your business?
A. I am involved in the residential aspect of design. I have done some (5 percent) contract design. I have done traditional, contemporary, eclectic, French country, and European "look" and showcase houses.

Q. Why did you decide to become an interior designer?

A. I decided to become an interior designer because I have had a love of design since sixth grade. I was a young mom with a college degree and decided to go back to school part time for interior design when my kids were young. I wanted a career that would afford me to continue as a mom first and then introduce myself to interior design. It took off!

Q. What do you like most and least about your job?

A. I love the creativity and people contact the most. What I like least are people who are afraid of losing control in a project and have a hard time trusting the designer. I think this is a universal problem with designers. It is hard to dig into the depths of creativity.

Q. What advice would you give to high school students who are interested in becoming interior designers?

A. My advice to high school students who may be interested in interior design is to try and get an internship with a design group or firm and join a student chapter of the American Society of Interior Designers.

Q. What are the three most important professional qualities for interior designers?

A. The three most important professional qualities for an interior designer are honesty, integrity, and intuition. Honesty is important because I believe in telling the truth to a client and having the truth told to me. Integrity, because I need to have sound, moral principles to live in this world and do my work. Intuition, because I need to get into my customers' heads and actualize what they are trying to visualize and feel.

Q. What is the future employment outlook in the field?

A. I honestly do not know what the future employment outlook in this field will be like, but what I do know is that everyone wants to have a happy place to come home to.

Jewelers and Jewelry Repairers

OVERVIEW

Jewelers, sometimes known as *bench jewelers,* create, either from their own design or one by a design specialist, rings, necklaces, bracelets, and other jewelry out of gold, silver, or platinum. Jewelry repairers alter ring sizes, reset stones, and refashion old jewelry. Restringing beads and stones, resetting clasps and hinges, and mending breaks in ceramic and metal pieces also are aspects of jewelry repair. A few jewelers are also trained as *gemologists,* who examine, grade, and evaluate gems, or gem cutters, who cut, shape, and polish gemstones. Many jewelers also repair watches and clocks. There are about 52,100 jewelers employed in the United States.

HISTORY

People have always worn adornments of some type. Early cave dwellers fashioned jewelry out of shells or the bones, teeth, or claws of animals. Beads have been found in the graves of prehistoric peoples. During the Iron Age, jewelry was made of ivory, wood, or metal. Precious stones were bought and sold at least 4,000 years ago in ancient Babylon, and there was widespread trade in jewelry by the Phoenicians and others in the Mediterranean and Asia Minor. The ancient Greeks and Romans were particularly fond of gold. Excavations of ancient Egyptian civilization show extremely well-crafted jewelry. It was during this time, it is believed, that jewelers first combined gems with precious metals.

QUICK FACTS

School Subjects
Art
Technical/shop

Personal Skills
Artistic
Mechanical/manipulative

Work Environment
Primarily indoors
Primarily one location

Minimum Education Level
Apprenticeship or some postsecondary training

Salary Range
$19,000 to $32,940 to
$55,130+

Certification or Licensing
Voluntary

Outlook
More slowly than the average

DOT
700

GOE
N/A

NOC
7344

O*NET-SOC
51-9071.00, 51-9071.01,
51-9071.03, 51-9071.04,
51-9071.05, 51-9071.06

Many of the metals jewelers use today, such as gold, silver, copper, brass, and iron, were first discovered or used by ancient jewelers. During the Hashemite Empire, a court jeweler discovered iron while seeking a stronger metal to use in battles. During the Renaissance period in Europe, jewelers became increasingly skillful. Artists such as Botticelli and Cellini used gold and silver with precious stones of every sort to create masterpieces of the gold and silversmiths' trades. Jewelers perfected the art of enameling during this time.

Many skilled artisans brought their trades to colonial America. The first jewelers were watchmakers, silversmiths, and coppersmiths. In early America, a versatile craft worker might create a ring or repair the copper handle on a cooking pot. By the 1890s, New York City had emerged as a center of the precious metal jewelry industry. It became a center for the diamond trade as well as for other precious stones. The first jewelry store, as we know it today, opened at the turn of the 19th century.

By the early 20th century, machines were used to create jewelry, and manufacturing plants began mass production of costume jewelry. These more affordable items quickly became popular and made jewelry available to large numbers of people.

New York City continues today as a leading center of the precious metals industry and jewelry manufacturing in the United States. Along with Paris and London, New York is a prime location for many fine jewelry designers.

During the 1980s, a small niche of jewelers began creating their own designs and either making them themselves or having other jewelers fabricate them. Also called *jewelry artists,* they differ from more traditional designers both in the designs they create and the methods and materials they use. They sell their designer lines of jewelry in small boutiques, galleries, or at crafts shows or market them to larger retail stores. Many of these jewelers open their own stores.

The American Jewelry Design Council was founded in 1988 to help promote designer jewelry as an art form.

THE JOB

Jewelers may design, make, sell, or repair jewelry. Many jewelers combine two or more of these skills. Designers conceive and sketch ideas for jewelry that they may make themselves or have made by another craftsperson. The materials used by the jeweler and the jewelry repairer may be precious, semiprecious, or synthetic. They work with valuable stones such as diamonds and rubies, and precious metals such as gold, silver, and platinum. Some jewelers use synthetic stones in their jewelry to make items more affordable.

The jeweler begins by forming an item in wax or metal with carving tools. The jeweler then places the wax model in a casting ring and pours plaster into the ring to form a mold. The mold is inserted into a furnace to melt the wax and a metal model is cast from the plaster mold. The jeweler pours the precious molten metal into the mold or uses a centrifugal casting machine to cast the article. Cutting, filing, and polishing are final touches the jeweler makes to a piece.

Jewelers do most of their work sitting down. They use small hand and machine tools, such as drills, files, saws, soldering irons, and jewelers' lathes. They often wear an eye loupe, or magnifying glass. They constantly use their hands and eyes and need good finger and hand dexterity.

Most jewelers specialize in creating certain kinds of jewelry or focus on a particular operation, such as making, polishing, or stone-setting models and tools. Specialists include gem cutters; stone setters; fancy-wire drawers; locket, ring, and hand chain makers; and sample makers.

Silversmiths design, assemble, decorate, or repair silver articles. They may specialize in one or more areas of the jewelry field such as repairing, selling, or appraising. *Jewelry engravers* carve text or graphic decorations on jewelry. *Watchmakers* repair, clean, and adjust mechanisms of watches and clocks.

Gem and diamond workers select, cut, shape, polish, or drill gems and diamonds using measuring instruments, machines, or hand tools. Some work as diamond die polishers, while others are gem cutters.

Other jewelry workers perform such operations as precision casting and modeling of molds, or setting precious and semiprecious stones for jewelry. They may make gold or silver chains and cut designs or lines in jewelry using hand tools or cutting machines. Other jewelers work as pearl restorers or jewelry bench hands.

Assembly line methods are used to produce costume jewelry and some types of precious jewelry, but the models and tools needed for factory production must be made by highly skilled jewelers. Some molds and models for manufacturing are designed and created using computer-aided design/manufacturing systems. Costume jewelry often is made by a die-stamping process. In general, the more precious the metals, the less automated the manufacturing process.

About 54 percent of jewelers and jewelry repairers are self-employed; others work for manufacturing and retail establishments. Workers in a manufacturing plant include skilled, semiskilled, and unskilled positions. Skilled positions include jewelers, ring makers, engravers, toolmakers, electroplaters, and stone cutters and setters. Semiskilled positions include polishers, repairers, toolsetters, and solderers. Unskilled workers are press operators, carders, and linkers.

Jewelers must be very attentive to detail and have good hand–eye coordination. *(Michael Sofronski, The Image Works)*

Books to Read

Ball, Joanne Dubbs. *Costume Jewelers: The Golden Age of Design.* 3d ed. Atglen, Pa.: Schiffer Publishing, Ltd., 2000.

Codina, Carles. *The Complete Book of Jewelry Making: A Full-Color Introduction to the Jeweler's Art.* Asheville, N.C.: Lark Books, 2006.

Finlay, Victoria. *Jewels: A Secret History.* New York: Random House Trade Paperbacks, 2007.

Knuth, Bruce G. *Jeweler's Resource: A Reference of Gems, Metals, Formulas and Terminology for Jewelers.* Rev. ed. Thornton, Colo.: Jewelers Press, 2000.

McCreight, Tim. *Jewelry: Fundamentals of Metalsmithing.* Cincinnati, Ohio: North Light Books, 2003.

McGrath, Jinks. *The Complete Jewelry Making Course: Principles, Practice and Techniques: A Beginner's Course for Aspiring Jewelry Makers.* Barron's Educational Series, 2007.

Olver, Elizabeth. *Jewelry Design: The Artisan's Reference.* 2d ed. Cincinnati, Ohio: North Light Books, 2003.

Although some jewelers operate their own retail stores, an increasing number of jewelry stores are owned or managed by individuals who are not jewelers. In such instances, a jeweler or jewelry repairer may be employed by the owner, or the store may send its repairs to a trade shop operated by a jeweler who specializes in repair work. Jewelers who operate their own stores sell jewelry, watches, and, frequently, merchandise such as silverware, china, and glassware. Many retail jewelry stores are located in or near large cities, with the eastern section of the United States providing most of the employment in jewelry manufacturing.

Other jobs in the jewelry business include *gemologists,* who analyze, describe, and certify the quality of gemstones; *appraisers,* who examine jewelry and determine its value and quality; *sales workers,* who set up and care for jewelry displays, take inventory, and help customers; and *buyers,* who purchase jewelry, gems, and watches from wholesalers and resell the items to the public in retail stores.

REQUIREMENTS

High School

A high school diploma usually is necessary for those desiring to enter the jewelry trade. While you are in high school, take courses in chemistry, physics, mechanical drawing, and art. Computer-aided design classes will be especially beneficial to you if you are planning to design jewelry. Sculpture and metalworking classes will prepare you for design and repair work.

Postsecondary Training

A large number of educational and training programs are available in jewelry and jewelry repair. Trade schools and community colleges offer a variety of programs, including classes in basic jewelry-making skills, techniques, use and care of tools and machines, stone setting, casting, polishing, and gem identification. Programs usually run from six months to one year, although individual classes are shorter and can be taken without enrolling in an entire program.

Some colleges and universities offer programs in jewelry store management, metalwork, and jewelry design. You can also find classes at fashion institutes, art schools, and art museums. In addition, you can take correspondence courses and continuing education classes. For sales and managerial positions in a retail store, college experience is usually helpful. Recommended classes are sales techniques, gemology, advertising, accounting, business administration, and computers.

The work of the jeweler and jewelry repairer may also be learned through an apprenticeship or by informal on-the-job training. The latter often includes instruction in design, quality of precious stones, and chemistry of metals. The apprentice becomes a jeweler upon the successful completion of a two-year apprenticeship and passing written and oral tests covering the trade. The apprenticeship generally focuses on casting, stone setting, and engraving.

Most jobs in manufacturing require on-the-job training, although many employers prefer to hire individuals who have completed a technical education program.

Certification or Licensing

Certification is available in several areas through the Jewelers of America, a trade organization. Those who do bench work (the hands-on work creating and repairing jewelry) can be certified at one of four levels: certified bench jeweler technician, certified bench jeweler, certified senior bench jeweler, and certified master bench jeweler. Each certification involves passing a written test and a bench test. Jewelers of America also offers certification for management and sales workers. Although voluntary, these certifications show that a professional has met certain standards for the field and is committed to this work.

Other Requirements

Jewelers and jewelry repairers need to have extreme patience and skill to handle the expensive materials of the trade. Although the physically disabled may find employment in this field, superior hand-eye coordination is essential. Basic mechanical skills such as filing, sawing, and drilling are vital to the jewelry repairer. Jewelers who work from their own designs need creative and artistic ability. They also should have a strong understanding of metals and their properties. Retail jewelers and those who operate or own trade shops and manufacturing establishments must work well with people and have a knowledge of merchandising and business management and practices. Sales staff should be knowledgeable and friendly, and buyers must have good judgment, self-confidence, and leadership abilities. Because of the expensive nature of jewelry, some people working in the retail industry are bonded, which means they must pass the requirements for an insurance company to underwrite them.

EXPLORING

If you are interested in becoming a jeweler or jewelry repairer, you can become involved in arts and crafts activities and take classes in crafts and jewelry making. Many community education programs are available through high schools, park districts, or local art stores and museums. Hobbies such as metalworking and sculpture are useful in becoming familiar with metals and the tools jewelers use. Visits to museums and fine jewelry stores to see collections of jewelry can be helpful.

If you are interested in the retail aspect of this field, you should try to find work in a retail jewelry store on a part-time basis or during the summer. A job in sales, or even as a clerk, can provide a first-hand introduction to the business. A retail job will help you become familiar with a jewelry store's operations, its customers, and the jewelry sold. In addition, you will learn the terminology unique to the jewelry field. Working in a store with an in-house jeweler or jewelry repairer provides many opportunities to observe and speak with a professional engaged in this trade. In a summer or part-time job as a bench worker or assembly line worker in a factory, you may perform only a few of the operations involved in making jewelry, but you will be exposed to many of the skills used within a manufacturing plant.

You also may want to visit retail stores and shops where jewelry is made and repaired or visit a jewelry factory. Some boutiques and galleries are owned and operated by jewelers who enjoy the opportunity to talk to people about their trade. Art fairs and crafts shows where jewelers exhibit and sell their products provide a more relaxed environment where jewelers are likely to have time to discuss their work.

EMPLOYERS

Approximately 52,100 jewelers and precious stone and metal workers are employed in the United States. Jewelers work in a variety of settings, from production work in multinational corporations to jewelry stores and repair shops. Some jewelers specialize in gem and diamond work, watchmaking, jewelry appraisal, repair, or engraving, where they may work in manufacturing or at the retail level. Other jewelers work only as appraisers. In most cases, appraisals are done by store owners or jewelers who have years of experience. About 54 percent of all jewelers are self-employed, according to the U.S. Department of Labor. The majority of the self-employed jewelers own their own stores or repair shops or specialize in designing and creating custom jewelry. Top states for jewelry manufacturing include Rhode Island, New Mexico, New York, South Dakota, and Louisiana.

STARTING OUT

A summer or part-time job in a jewelry store or the jewelry department of a department store will help you learn about the business. Another way to enter this line of work is to contact jewelry manufacturing establishments in major production centers. A trainee can acquire the many skills needed in the jewelry trade. The number of trainees accepted in this manner, however, is relatively small. Students who have completed a training program improve their chances of finding work as an apprentice or trainee. Students may learn about available jobs and apprenticeships through the career services offices of training schools they attend, from local jewelers, or from the personnel offices of manufacturing plants.

Those desiring to establish their own retail businesses find it helpful to first obtain employment with an established jeweler or a manufacturing plant. Considerable financial investment is required to open a retail jewelry store, and jewelers in such establishments find it to their advantage to be able to do repair work on watches as well as the usual jeweler's work. Less financial investment is needed to open a trade shop. These shops generally tend to be more successful in or near areas with large populations where they can take advantage of the large volume of jewelry business. Both retail jewelry stores and trade shops are required to meet local and state business laws and regulations.

ADVANCEMENT

There are many opportunities for advancement in the jewelry field. Jewelers and jewelry repairers can go into business for themselves once they have mastered the skills of their trade. They may create their own designer lines of jewelry that they market and sell, or they can open a trade shop or retail store. Many self-employed jewelers gain immense satisfaction from the opportunity to specialize in one aspect of jewelry or to experiment with new methods and materials.

Workers in jewelry manufacturing have fewer opportunities for advancement than in other areas of jewelry because of the declining number of workers needed. Plant workers in semiskilled and unskilled positions can advance based on the speed and quality of their work and by perseverance. On-the-job training can provide opportunities for positions that require more skill. Workers in manufacturing who show proficiency can advance to supervisory and management positions, or they may leave manufacturing and go to work in a retail shop or trade shop.

The most usual avenue of advancement is from employee in a factory, shop, or store to owner or manager of a trade shop or retail store. Sales is an excellent starting place for people who want to own their own store. Sales staff receive firsthand training in customer relations as well as knowledge of the different aspects of jewelry store merchandising. Sales staff may become gem experts who are qualified to manage a store, and managers may expand their territory from one store to managing several stores in a district or region. Top management in retail offers many interesting and rewarding positions to people who are knowledgeable, responsible, and ambitious. Buyers may advance by dealing exclusively with fine gems that are more expensive, and some buyers become *diamond merchants,* buying diamonds on the international market.

Jewelry designers' success depends not only on the skill with which they make jewelry but also on the ability to create new designs and keep in touch with current trends in the consumer market. Jewelry designers attend crafts shows, trade shows, and jewelry exhibitions to see what others are making and to get ideas for new lines of jewelry.

EARNINGS

Jewelers and precious stone and metal workers had median annual earnings of $32,940 in 2008, according to the U.S. Department of Labor. Salaries ranged from less than $19,000 to more than $55,130. Most jewelers start out with a base salary. With experience, they can charge by the number of pieces completed. Jewelers who work in retail stores may earn a commission for each piece of jewelry sold, in addition to their base salary.

Most employers offer benefit packages that include paid holidays and vacations and health insurance. Retail stores may offer discounts on store purchases.

WORK ENVIRONMENT

Jewelers work in a variety of environments. Some self-employed jewelers design and create jewelry in their homes; others work in small studios or trade shops. Jewelers who create their own designer lines of jewelry may travel to retail stores and other sites to promote their merchandise. Many designers also attend trade shows and exhibitions to learn more about current trends. Some sell their jewelry at both indoor and outdoor art shows and craft fairs. These shows are held on weekends, evenings, or during the week. Many jewelry artists live and work near tourist areas or in art communities.

Workers in jewelry manufacturing plants usually work in clean, air-conditioned, and relatively quiet environments. Workers in departments such as polishing, electroplating, and lacquer spraying may be exposed to fumes from chemicals and solvents. Workers who do bench work sit at workstations. Other workers stand at an assembly line for many hours at a time. Many workers in a manufacturing plant perform only one or two types of operations so the work can become repetitive. Most employees in a manufacturing plant work 35-hour workweeks, with an occasional need for overtime.

Retail store owners, managers, jewelers, and sales staff work a variety of hours and shifts that include weekends, especially during the Christmas season, the busiest time of year. Buyers may work more than 40 hours a week because they must travel to see wholesalers. Work settings vary from small shops and boutiques to large department stores. Most jewelry stores are clean, quiet, pleasant, and attractive. However, most jewelry store employees spend many hours on their feet dealing with customers, and buyers travel a great deal.

OUTLOOK

Employment opportunities for jewelers are expected to grow more slowly than the average for all occupations through 2018, according to the *Occupational Outlook Handbook*. Despite this prediction, jewelers and jewelry repairers will continue to be needed to replace those workers who leave the workforce or move to new positions. Since jewelry sales are increasing at rates that exceed the number of new jewelers entering the profession, employers are finding it difficult to find skilled employees.

Consumers now are purchasing jewelry from mass marketers, discount stores, catalogs, television shopping shows, and the Internet as well as from traditional retail stores. This may result in store closings or limited hiring.

The number of workers in manufacturing plants is declining because of increased automation and offshoring of jewelry manufacturing. These developments will limit opportunities for less-skilled manufacturing workers.

Demand in retail is growing for people who are skilled in personnel, management, sales and promotion, advertising, floor and window display, and buying. Opportunities will be best for graduates of training programs for jewelers or gemologists.

FOR MORE INFORMATION

For answers to frequently asked questions about jewelry, visit the society's Web site.
American Gem Society
8881 West Sahara Avenue
Las Vegas, NV 89117-5865
Tel: 866-805-6500
http://www.americangemsociety.org

For information on designer jewelry, contact
American Jewelry Design Council
P.O. Box 4164
Boulder, CO 80306-4164
Tel: 800-376-3609
http://www.ajdc.org

For an information packet with tuition prices, application procedures, and course descriptions, contact
Gemological Institute of America
The Robert Mouawad Campus
5345 Armada Drive
Carlsbad, CA 92008-4602
Tel: 800-421-7250
http://www.gia.edu

For certification information, a school directory, and a copy of
Careers in the Jewelry Industry, *contact*
Jewelers of America

52 Vanderbilt Avenue, 19th Floor
New York, NY 10017-3827
Tel: 800-223-0673
E-mail: info@jewelers.org
http://www.jewelers.org

For career and school information, contact
Manufacturing Jewelers and Suppliers of America
57 John L. Dietsch Square
Attleboro Falls, MA 02763-1027
Tel: 800-444-6572
http://www.mjsa.org

Landscape Architects

OVERVIEW

Landscape architects plan and design areas such as highways, housing communities, college campuses, commercial centers, recreation facilities, and nature conservation areas. They work to balance beauty and function in developed outdoor areas. There are approximately 26,700 landscape architects employed in the United States.

HISTORY

In the United States, landscape architecture has been practiced as a profession for a little more than 100 years. During the early part of the 20th century, landscape architects were employed mainly by the wealthy or by the government on public-works projects. In 1918, the practice of dividing large plots of land into individual lots for sale was born. In addition, there was a new public interest in the development of outdoor recreational facilities. These two factors provided many new opportunities for landscape architects.

The most dramatic growth occurred following the environmental movement of the 1960s, when public respect for protection of valuable natural resources reached an all-time high. Landscape architects have played a key role in encouraging the protection of natural resources while providing for the increasing housing and recreation needs of the American public.

In the last 30 years, the development of recreational areas has become more important as has the development of streets, bypasses, and massive highways. Landscape architects are needed in most projects of this nature. They are also increasingly relied up on to offer consultation for green landscaping—for example, sustainable

QUICK FACTS

School Subjects
Agriculture
Art
Earth science

Personal Skills
Artistic
Technical/scientific

Work Environment
Indoors and outdoors
Primarily multiple locations

Minimum Education Level
Bachelor's degree

Salary Range
$36,520 to $58,960 to $97,370+

Certification or Licensing
Required by most states

Outlook
Much faster than the average

DOT
001

GOE
02.07.03

NOC
2151

O*NET-SOC
17-1012.00

garden or green spaces or for restoring once-natural areas to their original state. In short, the skills of landscape architects are needed now more than ever.

THE JOB

Landscape architects plan and design outdoor spaces that make the best use of the land and at the same time respect the needs of the natural environment. They may be involved in a number of different types of projects, including the design of parks or gardens, scenic roads, housing projects, college or high school campuses, country clubs, cemeteries, or golf courses. Both the public and private sectors employ them.

Landscape architects begin a project by carefully reviewing their client's desires, including the purpose, structures needed, and funds available. They study the work site itself, observing and mapping such features as the slope of the land, existing structures, plants, and trees. They also consider different views of the location, taking note of shady and sunny areas, the structure of the soil, and existing utilities.

Landscape architects consult with a number of different people, such as engineers, architects, city officials, zoning experts, planners, real estate agents and brokers, and landscape nursery workers to develop a complete understanding of the job. Then they develop detailed plans and drawings of the site to present to the client for approval. Some projects take many months before the proposed plans are ready to be presented to the client.

After developing final plans and drawing up a materials list, landscape architects invite construction companies to submit bids for the job. Depending upon the nature of the project and the contractual agreement, landscape architects may remain on the job to supervise construction, or they may leave the project once work has begun. Those who remain on the job serve as the client's representative until the job is completed and approved.

REQUIREMENTS

High School

To prepare for a college program in landscape architecture, you should take courses in English composition and literature; social sciences, including history, government, and sociology; natural sciences, including biology, chemistry, and physics; and mathematics. If available, take drafting and mechanical drawing courses to begin building the technical skills needed for the career.

A landscape architect (*left*) and an architect stand by drawings of the Anchorage Museum of History and Art expansion as they explain how a new bus stop would fit into a proposed birch tree forest and other designs as part of the expansion. *(Al Grillo, AP Photo)*

Postsecondary Training

A bachelor's or master's degree in landscape architecture is usually the minimum requirement for entry into this field. Undergraduate and graduate programs in landscape architecture are offered in various colleges and universities; 67 colleges and universities are accredited by the Landscape Architectural Accreditation Board of the American Society of Landscape Architects (ASLA). Courses of study usually focus on six basic areas of the profession: landscape design, landscape construction, plants, architecture, graphic expression (mechanical, freehand, and computer-based drawings), and verbal expression.

Hands-on work is a crucial element to the curriculum. Whenever possible, students work on real projects to gain experience with computer-aided design programs and multimedia simulation.

Certification or Licensing

In 2009, 49 states required landscape architects to be licensed. To obtain licensure, applicants must pass the Landscape Architect Registration Examination, sponsored by the Council of Landscape Architectural Registration Boards (CLARB). Though standards vary by state, most require applicants to have a degree from an accredited program and to be working toward one to four years of experience in the field. In addition, 13 states require prospective landscape architects to pass a state exam that tests knowledge of local environmental regulations, vegetation, and other characteristics unique to the particular state. Because these standards vary, landscape architects may have to reapply for licensure if they plan to work in a different state. However, in many cases, workers who meet the national standards and have passed the exam may be granted the right to work elsewhere. For more information on licensing, contact the CLARB (http://www.clarb.org) or the ASLA (http://www.asla.org).

Landscape architects working for the federal government need a bachelor's or master's degree but do not need to be licensed.

Other Requirements

You should be interested in art and nature and have good business sense, especially if you hope to work independently. Interest in environmental protection, community improvement, and landscape design is also crucial for the profession. You should also be flexible and be able to think creatively to solve unexpected problems that may develop during the course of a project.

EXPLORING

If you are interested in learning more about the field, you can gather information and experience in a number of ways. Apply for a summer internship with a landscape architectural firm or at least arrange to talk with someone in the job. Ask them questions about their daily duties, the job's advantages and disadvantages, and if they recommend any landscape architecture programs. Finally, you can take the Landscape Architecture Interest Test at the American Society of Landscape Architects Web site to gauge your interest in the profession (http://www.asla.org/ContentDetail.aspx?id=12732&PageTitle =Education&RMenuId=54).

EMPLOYERS

There are approximately 26,700 landscape architects employed in the United States. About 51 percent of landscape architects are employed in architectural, engineering, and related services and 6 percent work for state and local governments. Landscape architects work in every state in the United States, in small towns and cities as well as heavily populated areas. Some work in rural areas, such as those who plan and design parks and recreational areas. However the majority of positions are found in suburban and urban areas.

Landscape architects work for a variety of different employers in both the public and private sectors. They may work with a school board planning a new elementary or high school, with manufacturers developing a new factory, with homeowners improving the land surrounding their home, or with a city council planning a new suburban development.

In the private sector, most landscape architects do some residential work, though few limit themselves entirely to projects with individual homeowners. Larger commercial or community projects are usually more profitable. Workers in the public sector plan and design government buildings, parks, and public lands. They also may conduct studies on environmental issues and restore lands such as mines or landfills.

STARTING OUT

After graduating from a landscape architecture program, you can usually receive job assistance from your school's career services office. Although these services do not guarantee a job, they can be of great help in making initial contacts. Many positions are posted by the American Society of Landscape Architects and published in its two journals, *Landscape Architecture News Digest Online* (http://land.asla.org) and *Landscape Architecture* (http://archives.asla.org/nonmembers/lam.html). Government positions are normally filled through civil service examinations. Information regarding vacancies may be obtained through the local, state, or federal civil service commissions.

Most new hires are often referred to as interns or apprentices until they have gained initial experience in the field and have passed the necessary examinations. Apprentices' duties vary by employer; some handle background project research, others are directly involved in planning and design. Whatever their involvement, all new hires work under the direct supervision of a licensed landscape architect. All drawings and plans must be signed and sealed by the licensed supervisor for legal purposes.

ADVANCEMENT

After obtaining licensure and gaining work experience in all phases of a project's development, landscape architects can become project managers, responsible for overseeing the entire project and meeting schedule deadlines and budgets. They can also advance to the level of associate, increasing their earning opportunities by gaining a profitable stake in a firm.

The ultimate objective of many landscape architects is to gain the experience necessary to organize and open their own firm. According to the U.S. Department of Labor, approximately 21 percent of all landscape architects are self-employed—approximately two times the average of workers in other professions. After the initial investment in computer-aided design software, few start-up costs are involved in breaking into the business independently.

EARNINGS

Salaries for landscape architects vary depending on the employer, work experience, location, and whether they are paid a straight salary or earn a percentage of a firm's profits.

According to 2008 data from the U.S. Department of Labor, the median annual salary for landscape architects was $58,960. The lowest paid 10 percent earned less than $36,520 and the highest paid 10 percent earned more than $97,370. The average salary for those working for the federal government in 2008 was $80,380. Landscape architects employed by state and local governments had average annual salaries of $74,240 and $68,280, respectively.

Benefits also vary depending on the employer but usually include health insurance coverage, paid vacation time, and sick leave. Many landscape architects work for small landscaping firms or are self-employed. These workers generally receive fewer benefits than those who work for large organizations.

WORK ENVIRONMENT

Landscape architects spend much of their time in the field gathering information at the work site. They also spend time in the office, drafting plans and designs. Those working for larger organizations may have to travel farther away to reach worksites.

Work hours are generally regular, except during periods of increased business or when nearing a project deadline. Hours vary for self-employed workers because they determine their own schedules.

OUTLOOK

According to the *Occupational Outlook Handbook,* the employment of landscape architects is expected to increase much faster than the average for all occupations through 2018. The increase in demand for landscape architects is a result of several factors: growth of the construction industry, the availability of government funding for surface transportation and transit programs (such as interstate highway construction and maintenance and pedestrian and bicycle trails), the need to refurbish existing sites, and the increase in city and environmental planning and historic preservation. In addition, many job openings are expected to result from the need to replace experienced workers who leave the field. The U.S. Department of Labor predicts that, in the future, landscape architects will be needed to help "manage stormwater run-off to avoid pollution of waterways and conserve water resources...and preserve and restore wetlands and other environmentally sensitive sites."

The need for landscape architecture depends to a great extent on the construction industry. In the event of an economic downturn, when real estate transactions and the construction business is expected to drop off, opportunities for landscape architects will also dwindle.

Opportunities will be the greatest for workers who develop strong technical skills. The growing use of technology such as computer-aided design will not diminish the demand for landscape architects. New and improved techniques will be used to create better designs more efficiently rather than reduce the number of workers needed to do the job.

FOR MORE INFORMATION

For information on the career, accredited education programs, licensure requirements, and available publications, contact
American Society of Landscape Architects
636 Eye Street, NW
Washington, DC 20001-3736
Tel: 202-898-2444
E-mail: info@asla.org
http://www.asla.org

For information on student resources, license examinations, and continuing education, contact
Council of Landscape Architectural Registration Boards
3949 Pender Drive, Suite 120
Fairfax, VA 22030-6088
Tel: 571-432-0332
http://www.clarb.org

For career and educational information, visit
Landscape Architecture
http://www.laprofession.org

INTERVIEW

Susan Kill Kegan, RLA, is a landscape architect. She discussed her career with the editors of Careers in Focus: Design.

Q. How long have you worked in the field? Can you tell us a little about your professional background and job duties?

A. Thirty years! For 23 years I was able to have the best of both worlds as a self-employed landscape architect with a home office. I had a flexible work schedule while making a good hourly wage while raising my three children.

My current employer saw the value in hiring an experienced, skilled person to add to her relatively younger staff. My current job duties include project management—from client call to design to construction closeout.

Q. What do you like least and most about being a landscape architect?

A. There have been times when I've felt that the profession has not been taken seriously by architects and engineers. Often I have been called to "fill in the plants" when the job could have benefited from an earlier intervention. What I like most now is the collaboration with others after being self-employed for so long.

Q. What are the most important personal and professional qualities for landscape architects?

A. Landscape architects should have a love for art and the environment. This profession combines aspects of both science and design with professional practices of marketing, sales, writing proposals, customer service skills, and business administration.

Q. What advice would you give to young people who are seeking to enter this career?

A. There are many opportunities opening up for all things "green"—green roofs, rain gardens, bioswales, etc., and general infrastructure design and construction.

Makeup Artists

OVERVIEW

Makeup artists prepare actors for performances on stage and before cameras. They read scripts and consult with directors, producers, and technicians to design makeup effects for each individual character. They apply makeup and prosthetics and build and style wigs. They also create special makeup effects. Approximately 2,800 theatrical and performance makeup artists are employed in the United States.

HISTORY

Theatrical makeup is as old as the theater itself. Cultures around the world performed ritualistic dances, designed by spiritual leaders, to communicate with gods and other supernatural forces. These dances often involved elaborate costumes and makeup. By the Elizabethan age, theater had become an entertainment requiring special makeup techniques to transform the male actors into female characters. In Asia in the 17th century, Kabuki theater maintained the symbolic origins of the drama; actors wore very stylized makeup to depict each character's nature and social standing. It was not until the late 18th century in Europe that plays, and therefore costumes and makeup, were based on realistic portrayals of society. The grease stick, a special makeup stick that could withstand harsh stage lights without smearing, was invented in the 19th century.

This grease stick led the way for other advancements in the chemistry of stage makeup, but even today's makeup artists must use ingenuity and invention to create special effects. With the advent of filmmaking came new challenges in makeup design—artists were

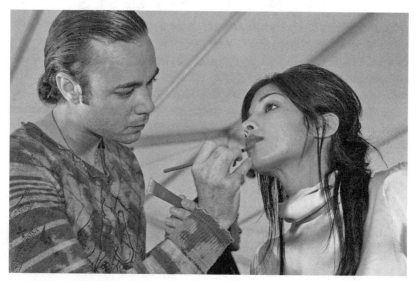

A makeup artist applies makeup to a model before a fashion show. *(Jeff Greenberg, The Image Works)*

required to create makeup that would not only hold up under intense lighting, but would look realistic close up. The silent film star Lon Chaney was a pioneer in makeup effects; his dedication to the craft was so extreme that he permanently injured himself with the restrictive prosthetics he used in *The Hunchback of Notre Dame* in 1923. His gruesome makeup design for *The Phantom of the Opera* in 1925 set a standard for all horror films to follow; today, the horror genre has inspired some of the most inventive and memorable makeup effects in film history.

THE JOB

Makeup artists apply makeup and other material to performers. They often create elaborate facial decorations to depict age, scars, or injuries. Makeup artists also apply "clean" makeup, which is a technique of applying foundations and powders to keep actors and models looking natural under the harsh lighting of stage and film productions. Makeup artists accent, or downplay, an actor's natural features. They conceal an actor's scars, skin blemishes, tattoos, and wrinkles, as well as apply these things when needed for the character.

Makeup artists who work on films, television shows, and music videos must do a lot more than just apply makeup. First, they must read the script and meet with the director and technicians to learn about the project and the characters in it. Makeup artists take into consideration many factors: the age of the characters, the setting of the production, the time period, lighting effects, and other details that determine how an actor should appear. Historical productions require a great deal of research to learn about the hair and clothing styles of the time. Makeup artists also style hair; apply wigs, bald caps, beards, and sideburns; and temporarily color hair. In many states, however, makeup artists are limited in the hair services they can perform; some productions bring in locally licensed cosmetologists for hair cutting, dye jobs, and perms.

After much preparation, the makeup artist becomes an important backstage presence during a production. Throughout the making of a film or television show, makeup artists arrive early for work every day. Makeup artists are required to maintain the actors' proper makeup throughout filming and to help the actors remove the makeup at the end of the day. With the aid of fluorescent lighting, makeup artists apply the makeup, and they keep their eyes on the monitors during filming to make sure the makeup looks right.

Most makeup artists for film and television are in business for themselves, contracting work from studios, production companies, and special effects houses on a freelance basis. They may supplement their film and television work with projects for video, commercials, industrial films, and photo shoots for professional photographers. Makeup artists for theater may also work freelance or be employed full-time by a theater or theater troupe. Makeup artists for theater find work with regional theaters, touring shows, and recreational parks.

REQUIREMENTS

High School
Does becoming a makeup artist sound interesting to you? If so, there are a number of classes you can take in high school to help prepare for this profession. Take all the art classes you can, including art history if this is offered at your school. Photography courses will help you understand the use of light and shadow. Courses in illustration, painting, and drawing will help you to develop the skills you'll need for illustrating proposed makeup effects. Learning about sculpting is important, as creating special makeup effects with rubber, prosthetics, and glue is often much like sculpting from clay. Other helpful classes for you to take are anatomy and chemistry. Anatomy will give you an understanding of the human body, and chemistry will give you insight into the products you will be using. If your school offers drama classes, be sure to take these. In drama class you will gain an understanding of all the different elements—such as scripts, actors, and location—needed for a production. Computer classes will give you

exposure to this technology, which you may use in the future to design projects. Try experimenting with makeup and special effects on your own. Take photographs of your efforts in order to build a portfolio of your work. Finally, because this work is typically done on a freelance basis and you will need to manage your business accounts, it will be helpful to take math, business, and accounting classes.

Postsecondary Training

There are a number of postsecondary educational routes you can take to become a makeup artist. If you have experience and a portfolio to show off your work, you may be able to enter the business right out of high school. This route is not always advisable, however, because your chances for establishing a successful freelance career without further training are slim. You must be very ambitious, enthusiastic, and capable of seeking out successful mentors willing to teach you the ropes. This can mean a lot of time working for free or for very little pay.

Another route you can take is to get specific training for makeup artistry through vocational schools. One advantage of this route is that after graduating from the program, you will be able to use the school's career services office, instructors, and other graduates as possible networking sources for jobs. Probably the most highly respected schools for makeup artists in film are the Joe Blasco Makeup Schools, which have several locations across the country. Topics you might study at a Joe Blasco school include beauty makeup, old age makeup, bald cap, hairwork, and monster makeup. Some people in the business have cosmetology degrees, also offered by vocational schools. A cosmetology course of study, however, is not typically geared toward preparing you for makeup artistry work in the entertainment industry.

A third route you can take is to get a broad-based college or university education that results in either a bachelor's or master's degree. Popular majors for makeup artists include theater, art history, film history, photography, and fashion merchandising. In addition to makeup courses, it is important to take classes in painting, illustration, computer design, and animation. A master of fine arts degree in theater or filmmaking will allow you to gain hands-on experience in production as well as working with a faculty of practicing artists.

Certification or Licensing

In some states, makeup artists who also style hair must be licensed. Check with the state in which you plan to practice as a makeup artist for the specific laws and licensing requirements for hair stylists.

Other Requirements

Patience and the ability to get along well with people are important for a makeup artist—throughout a film production, the actors will spend many hours in the makeup chair. Though many actors will be easy to work with, you may have to put up with much irritability, as well as overwhelming egos. Producers and directors can also be difficult to work with. And, as you gain more experience, you may have more knowledge about filmmaking than some of the producers of the projects. This may put you in frustrating situations, and you may see time wasted in costly mistakes.

Attention to detail is important; you must be quick to spot any makeup problems before they are filmed. Such responsibilities can be stressful—a whole production team will be relying on you to properly apply makeup that will look good on film. If your work isn't up to par, the whole production will suffer. Work as a makeup artist requires as much creativity and ingenuity as any other film-making task. The directors and actors rely on the makeup artists to come up with interesting makeup effects and solutions to filming problems. Because of the tough, competitive nature of the entertainment industry, makeup artists must be persistent and enthusiastic in their pursuit of work.

As a makeup artist, you may want to consider joining a union. The International Alliance of Theatrical Stage Employees, Moving Picture Technicians, Artists and Allied Crafts of the United States, Its Territories, and Canada represents workers in theater, film, and television production. Hair stylists, makeup artists, engineers, art directors, and set designers are some of the professionals who belong to the local unions affiliated with the alliance. Union membership is not required of most makeup artists for film and theater, but it can help individuals negotiate better wages, benefits, and working conditions. Theaters in larger cities may require union membership of makeup artists, while smaller, regional theaters across the country are less likely to require membership.

EXPLORING

High school drama departments or local community theaters can provide you with great opportunities to explore the makeup artist's work. Volunteer to assist with makeup during a stage production and you will learn about the materials and tools of a makeup kit, as well as see your work under stage lights. A high school video production team or film department may also offer you opportunities for makeup experience.

Most states have their own film commissions that are responsible for promoting film locales and inviting film productions to the local area. These film commissions generally need volunteers and may have internships for students. By working for a film commission, you will learn about productions coming to your state and may have the chance to work on the production. Film industry publications such as *Variety* (http://www.variety.com) can alert you to internship opportunities.

The summer is a great time for students interested in stage production to gain firsthand experience. There are probably local productions in your area, but summer theaters often promote positions nationally. The Theatre Communications Group publishes a directory of nonprofit professional theaters across the country. Its electronic publication, *ARTSEARCH,* provides information on summer theater positions and internships.

Finally, explore this career by reading other publications for the field. For example, check out *Make-Up Artist Magazine* (http://www.makeupmag.com), a bimonthly publication with profiles of makeup artists for film as well as how-to columns and product information. Another interesting publication is *The Artisan,* which is published by the Make-Up Artists & Hair Stylists Guild. Visit http://www.local706.org/artisan.cfm to read past issues.

EMPLOYERS

Approximately 2,800 theatrical and performance makeup artists are employed in the United States.

Although makeup artists work in a wide variety of circumstances, from theater to television to movies, they usually are self-employed, contracting individual jobs. Theater troupes, touring shows, and amusement parks may hire makeup artists on to their staffs, but in the film industry, makeup artists work on a freelance basis. Large cities and metropolitan areas will provide the majority of jobs for makeup artists, particularly those cities associated with thriving theaters, movie or television studios, fashion photography, and modeling/talent agencies. Although there may be some jobs in smaller towns, they probably will be mostly along the lines of industrial films, corporate videos, and photographic shoots—not very promising for those who wish to make a living in this line of work. Those who aspire to work exclusively as makeup artists gravitate toward the big cities.

STARTING OUT

You should keep a photographic record of all the work you do for theater and film productions, including photos of any drawings or sculptures you have done for art classes. It's important to have a portfolio to send along with your resume to effects shops, makeup departments, and producers. To build a portfolio of photographs, experiment in art classes and at home with makeup and special effects, and photograph the results. Check with local TV studios about work in their makeup departments. Locally produced newscasts, children's programming, documentaries, and commercials offer opportunities for makeup artists. Commercials are often quick productions (between one and three days) with small casts, and they pay well. Department stores hire makeup artists to demonstrate and sell cosmetic products in department stores, which may be a starting position for those who want to earn a salary while getting on-the-job training and practice.

Because of the freelance nature of the business, you will be going from project to project. This requires you to constantly seek out work. Read industry trade magazines like *Variety,* and don't be shy about submitting your portfolio to producers and studios. Self-promotion will be an important part of your success as a makeup artist.

ADVANCEMENT

Many makeup artists start as assistants or volunteers on a production, making contacts and connections. They eventually take on projects for which they are in charge of makeup departments and designing makeup effects. They may also establish their own production companies and make their own films or stage their own plays.

Successful, experienced makeup artists can pick and choose their projects and work as much as they like. In the early years, makeup artists must frequently take on a variety of different projects just for the money; however, as they become established in the field and develop a solid reputation, they can concentrate on projects specific to their interests.

EARNINGS

Makeup artists usually contract with a production, negotiating a daily rate. This rate can vary greatly from project to project, depending on the budget of the production, the prestige of the project, and other factors. Even well-established makeup artists occasionally forgo payment to work on the low-budget independent productions of filmmakers they respect.

Independent contractors don't draw steady, yearly salaries. This means they may work long hours for several weeks, then, upon completion of a production, go without work for several weeks.

Unless makeup artists are part of the union, they may have to provide all their own health insurance. An experienced makeup artist can make around $300 a day on a film with a sizable budget; some of the top makeup artists in the business command around $1,000 a day. Theatrical makeup artists can make comparable daily wages on Broadway, or in a theater in a large city; some small theaters, however, may only pay around $50 a day.

Because of such variables as the unsteady nature of the work, the makeup artist's experience, and even where he or she works, the yearly incomes for these individuals vary widely. Some makeup artists may show yearly earnings little higher than those resulting from the minimum wage. Others may have annual income in the hundreds of thousands of dollars. The U.S. Department of Labor reports that makeup artists, theatrical and performance had median salaries of $26,270 in 2008. Salaries ranged from less than $16,050 to more than $80,630. Salaried makeup artists working in the motion picture and video industries were among the highest paid, with annual median earnings of $79,600 in 2008. Those working in radio and television had annual median annual earnings of $40,720, and makeup artists working for performing arts companies received median salaries of $53,930.

WORK ENVIRONMENT

Long hours, deadlines, and tight budgets can result in high stress on a movie set. Because makeup artists move from production to production, they work with different groups of people all the time, and in different locales and settings. Although this allows makeup artists the opportunity to travel, it may also make a makeup artist feel displaced. While working on a production, they may have to forgo a social life, working long hours to design effects and prepare the actors for filming. The workdays may be twice as long as in the average workplace, and those work hours may be a stressful combination of working hurriedly then waiting.

When working for the theater, the conditions are generally more controlled. With the exception of outdoor productions, theatrical makeup artists work in the dressing and makeup rooms of theaters and concert halls. The work can be very stressful, however, as the actors hurry to prepare for live productions.

OUTLOOK

Makeup artists will find their opportunities increasing in the film and television industries. Digital TV has made it possible for hundreds of cable channels to be piped into our homes. The original programming needed to fill the schedules of these new channels results in jobs for makeup artists. Makeup effects artists will find challenging and well-paying work as the film industry pushes the envelope on special effects. These makeup artists may be using computers more and more, as digital design becomes an important tool in creating film effects.

Funding for theaters, some of which comes from the National Endowment for the Arts, is always limited and may be reduced during economic downturns or when productions are unpopular. During these times many theaters may be unable to hire the cast and crew needed for new productions. There has been a revived interest in Broadway, however, due to highly successful musicals like *Rent*, *The Lion King, and Wicked*. This interest could result in better business for traveling productions, as well as regional theaters across the country.

There will be a continuing need for makeup artists in still photography to prepare models for catalog and magazine shoots.

FOR MORE INFORMATION

For information on the alliance, a union representing more than 110,000 members in entertainment and related fields in the United States and Canada, contact

International Alliance of Theatrical Stage Employees, Moving Picture Technicians, Artists and Allied Crafts of the United States, Its Territories, and Canada
1430 Broadway, 20th Floor
New York, NY 10018-3348
Tel: 212-730-1770
http://www.iatse-intl.org

For information about the Joe Blasco schools and careers in makeup artistry, visit
Joe Blasco Makeup Schools
http://www.joeblasco.com

This local union of the International Alliance of Theatrical Stage Employees, Moving Picture Technicians, Artists and Allied Crafts of the United States, Its Territories, and Canada represents the professional Interests of makeup artists and hair stylists who work in film and television. Visit its Web site for more information.
Make-Up Artists & Hair Stylists Guild Local 706
http://www.local706.org

For information about theater jobs and ARTSEARCH, *contact*
Theatre Communications Group
520 Eighth Avenue, 24th Floor
New York, NY 10018-4156
Tel: 212-609-5900
E-mail: tcg@tcg.org
http://www.tcg.org

Merchandise Displayers

OVERVIEW

Merchandise displayers, sometimes known as *visual merchandisers,* design and install displays of clothing, accessories, furniture, and other products to attract customers. They set up these displays in windows and showcases and on the sales floors of retail stores. Display workers who specialize in dressing mannequins are known as *model dressers.* Those who specialize in installing displays in store windows are known as *window dressers* or *window trimmers.* These workers use their artistic flair and imagination to create excitement and customer interest in the store. They also work with other types of merchandising to develop exciting images, product campaigns, and shopping concepts. There are approximately 85,200 merchandise displayers and window trimmers employed in the United States.

HISTORY

Eye-catching displays of merchandise attract customers and encourage them to buy. This form of advertising has been used throughout history. Farmers in the past who displayed their produce at markets were careful to place their largest, most tempting fruits and vegetables at the top of the baskets. Peddlers opened their bags and cases and arranged their wares in attractive patterns. Store owners decorated their windows with collections of articles they hoped to sell. Their business success often was a matter of chance, however, and depended heavily on their own persuasiveness and sales ability.

As glass windows became less expensive, storefronts were able to accommodate larger window frames. This exposed more of the store to passersby, and stores soon found that decorative window displays were effective in attracting customers. Today, a customer may see nearly the entire store and the displays of the products it sells just by looking in the front window.

The advent of self-service stores has minimized the importance of the salesperson's personal touch. The merchandise now has to sell itself. Displays have become an important inducement for customers to buy. Advertising will bring people into stores, but an appealing product display can make the difference between a customer who merely browses and one who buys.

Merchandise displayers are needed year-round, but during the Christmas season they often execute their most elaborate work. Small retail stores generally depend on the owner or manager to create the merchandise displays, or they may hire a freelance window dresser on a part-time basis. Large retail operations, such as department stores, retain a permanent staff of display and visual merchandising specialists. Competition among these stores is intense, and their success depends on capturing a significant portion of the market. Therefore, they allocate a large share of their publicity budget to creating unique, captivating displays.

THE JOB

Using their imagination and creative ability, as well as their knowledge of color harmony, composition, and other fundamentals of art and interior design, merchandise displayers in retail establishments create an idea for a setting designed to show off merchandise and attract customers' attention. Often the display is planned around a theme or concept. After the display manager approves the design or idea, the display workers create the display. They install background settings, such as carpeting, wallpaper, and lighting, gather props and other accessories, arrange mannequins and merchandise, and place price tags and descriptive signs where they are needed.

Displayers may be assisted in some of these tasks by carpenters, painters, or store maintenance workers. Displayers may use merchandise from various departments of the store or props from previous displays. Sometimes they borrow special items that their business doesn't carry from other stores; for example, toys or sports equipment. The displays are dismantled and new ones are installed every few weeks. In very large stores that employ many display workers, displayers may specialize in carpentry, painting, making signs, or setting up interior or window displays. A *display director* usually supervises and coordinates the display workers' activities and confers with other managers to select merchandise to be featured.

Ambitious and talented display workers have many possible career avenues. The importance of visual merchandising is being recognized more and more as retail establishments compete for consumer dollars. Some display workers can advance to display director or even a position in store planning.

In addition to traditional stores, the skills of visual marketing workers are now in demand in many other types of establishments. Restaurants often try to present a distinct image to enhance the dining experience. Outlet stores, discount malls, and entertainment centers also use visual marketing to establish their identities with the public. Chain stores often need to make changes in or redesign all their stores and turn to display professionals for their expertise. Consumer product manufacturers also are heavily involved in visual marketing. They hire display and design workers to come up with exciting concepts, such as in-store shops, that present a unified image of the manufacturer's products and are sold as complete units to retail stores.

There are also opportunities for employment with store fixture manufacturers. Many companies build and sell specialized props, banners, signs, displays, and mannequins and hire display workers as sales representatives to promote their products. The display workers' understanding of retail needs and their insight into the visual merchandising industry make them valuable consultants.

Commercial decorators prepare and install displays and decorations for trade and industrial shows, exhibitions, festivals, and other special events. Working from blueprints, drawings, computer-generated designs, and floor plans, they use woodworking power tools to construct installations (usually referred to as booths) at exhibition halls and convention centers. They install carpeting, drapes, and other decorations, such as flags, banners, and lights. They arrange furniture and accessories to attract the people attending the exhibition. Special event producers, coordinators, and party planners may also seek out the skills of display professionals.

This occupation appeals to imaginative, artistic individuals who find it rewarding to use their creative abilities to visualize a design concept and transform it into reality. Original, creative displays grow out of an awareness of current design trends and popular themes. Although display workers use inanimate objects such as props and

Books to Read

Bell, Judith A. *Silent Selling: Best Practices And Effective Strategies in Visual Merchandising.* 3d ed. New York: Fairchild Books, 2006.

Diamond, Jay. *Contemporary Visual Merchandising and Environmental Design.* 4th ed. Upper Saddle River, N.J.: Prentice Hall, 2006.

Falk, Edgar A. *1001 Ideas to Create Retail Excitement.* Rev. ed. Upper Saddle River, N.J.: Prentice Hall Press, 2003.

Morgan, Tony. *Visual Merchandising: Windows and In-Store Displays for Retail.* London, U.K.: Laurence King Publishing, 2008.

Pegler, Martin M. *Visual Merchandising & Display.* 5th ed. New York: Fairchild Books, 2006.

Tucker, Johnny. *Retail Desire: Design Display and Visual Merchandising.* East Sussex, U.K.: RotoVision, 2003.

materials, an understanding of human motivations helps them create displays with strong customer appeal.

REQUIREMENTS

High School

To work as a display worker, you must have at least a high school diploma. Important high school subjects include art, woodworking, mechanical drawing, and merchandising.

Postsecondary Training

Some employers require college courses in art, interior decorating, fashion design, advertising, or related subjects. Community and junior colleges that offer advertising and marketing courses may include display work in the curriculum. Fashion merchandising schools and fine arts institutes also offer courses useful to display workers.

Much of the training for display workers is gained on the job. They generally start as helpers for routine tasks, such as carrying props and dismantling sets. Gradually they are permitted to build simple props and work up to constructing more difficult displays. As they become more experienced, display workers who show artistic talent may be assigned to plan simple designs. The total training time varies depending on the beginner's ability and the variety and complexity of the displays.

Other Requirements

Besides education and experience, you will also need creative ability, manual dexterity, and mechanical aptitude to do this work. You should possess the strength and physical ability needed to be able to carry equipment and climb ladders. You also need agility to work in close quarters without upsetting the props.

EXPLORING

To explore the work of merchandise displayers, try to get a part-time or summer job with a department or retail store or at a convention center. This will give you an overview of the display operations in these establishments. Photographers and theater groups need helpers to work with props and sets, although some may require previous experience or knowledge related to their work. You school's drama and photo clubs may offer opportunities to learn basic design concepts. You also should read about this line of work; *Display & Design Ideas* (http://www.ddimagazine.com) publishes articles on the field and related subjects.

EMPLOYERS

Approximately 85,200 merchandise displayers and window trimmers are employed in the United States. Most work in department and clothing stores, but many are employed in other types of retail stores, such as variety, drug, and shoe stores. Some have their own design businesses, and some are employed by design firms that handle interior and professional window dressing for small stores. Employment of display workers is distributed throughout the country, with most of the jobs concentrated in large towns and cities.

STARTING OUT

High school and college career services offices may have job listings for display workers or related positions. Individuals wishing to become display workers can apply directly to retail stores, decorating firms, or exhibition centers. Openings also may be listed in the classified ads of newspapers.

A number of experienced merchandise displayers choose to work as freelance designers. Competition in this area, however, is intense, and it takes time to establish a reputation, build a list of clients, and earn an adequate income. Freelancing part time while holding down another job provides a more secure income for many display workers. Freelancing also provides beginners with opportunities to develop a portfolio of photographs of their best designs, which they can then use to sell their services to other stores.

ADVANCEMENT

Display workers with supervisory ability can become regional managers. Further advancement may lead to a position as a display director or head of store planning.

Another way to advance is by starting a freelance design business. This can be done with very little financial investment, although freelance design workers must spend many long hours generating new business and establishing a reputation in the field.

Experienced display workers also may be able to transfer their skills to jobs in other art-related fields, such as interior design or photography. This move, however, requires additional training.

EARNINGS

According to the U.S. Department of Labor, the median annual earnings of merchandise displayers were $25,940 in 2008. The lowest paid 10 percent earned less than $17,380 and the highest paid 10 percent earned more than $42,590. Displayers working in department stores earned a mean salary of $27,630 in 2008, and those employed by clothing stores earned mean salaries of $28,280. Industries that pay the highest annual mean salaries are travel arrangement and reservation services, $46,020, and apparel, piece goods, and notions merchant wholesalers, $40,750.

Freelance displayers may earn more than $50,000 a year, but their income depends entirely on their talent, reputation, number of clients, and amount of time they work.

Merchandise displayers usually receive benefits such as vacation days, sick leave, health and life insurance, and a savings and pension program. Self-employed displayers must provide their own benefits.

WORK ENVIRONMENT

Display workers usually work 35 to 40 hours a week, except during busy seasons, such as Christmas. Selling promotions and increased sales drives during targeted seasons can require the display staff to work extra hours in the evening and on weekends.

The work of constructing and installing displays requires prolonged standing, bending, stooping, and working in awkward positions. There is some risk of falling off ladders or being injured from handling sharp materials or tools, but serious injuries are uncommon.

OUTLOOK

Employment for display workers is expected to grow about as fast as the average for all occupations through 2018, according to the U.S. Department of Labor. Growth in this profession is expected due to an expanding retail sector and the increasing popularity of visual merchandising. Most openings will occur as older, experienced workers retire or leave the occupation.

Fluctuations in our nation's economy affect the volume of retail sales because people are less likely to spend money during recessionary times. For display workers this can result in layoffs or hiring freezes.

FOR MORE INFORMATION

For information on membership for college students, scholarship opportunities, colleges with student chapters, and additional career materials, contact
American Society of Interior Designers
608 Massachusetts Avenue, NE
Washington, DC 20002-6006
Tel: 202-546-3480
http://www.asid.org

For membership information, contact
Retail Design Institute
25 North Broadway
Tarrytown, NY 10591-3221
Tel: 914-332-0040
E-mail: info@retaildesigninstitute.org
http://www.retaildesigninstitute.org

Packaging Designers

QUICK FACTS

School Subjects
Art
Computer science

Personal Skills
Artistic
Mechanical/manipulative

Work Environment
Primarily indoors
Primarily one location

Minimum Education Level
Bachelor's degree

Salary Range
$26,110 to $42,400 to
$74,660+

Certification or Licensing
None available

Outlook
About as fast as the average

DOT
141

GOE
01.04.02

NOC
5241

O*NET-SOC
27-1024.00

OVERVIEW

Packaging designers design product packaging and related materials. They often work with packaging engineers, product managers, and marketing and sales personnel to design packages that not only protect the product but also present the product in a manner that is visually pleasing and adds to its marketability.

HISTORY

Art has been around since before the first drawings on cave walls. Historically, there has been a need for people to express themselves creatively through the use of pictures, graphics, and words. This means of expression remains a vital part of today's manufacturing and marketing.

All product packaging has been influenced by the elements of design. From the labels on soup cans to the cans holding the soup, packaging designers work to create "the look" that they hope will entice consumers and bring in sales. Designers are responsible for the placement of corporate logos on all items that we recognize at a glance. Their graphic work builds brand-name recognition and consumer loyalty.

Old packaging designs can illustrate the evolution of this field. Soda that was once packaged in curvy glass bottles is now sold in similarly curvy plastic bottles and smaller aluminum cans. Older product labeling generally uses less color and graphics. Today's packaging designers use endless amounts of images and colors to advertise and promote their products. Although designers now use computers to help them create designs, creativity, imagination, and ingenuity must still drive the artistic process.

THE JOB

Packaging designers usually work in plants of various industries or for a company that contracts for package design services. They usually work with a team of employees to design and implement the packaging for products.

Typically, the designer meets with the product manager, the packaging engineer, the copywriter, and the marketing manager to determine the type of package to be produced, safety and storage issues, and the intended market. The designer must consider all of these factors to determine the final product weight and size, packaging production methods, design elements (such as logo, product pictures, instructions), labeling requirements (such as ingredients or warnings), and the method of shipment and storage. The designer then designs the packaging and graphics by using traditional design methods and computer-aided design software. Packaging ideas are usually presented to the product manager or before a committee for feedback. Prototypes may be developed and analyzed.

When a packaging design is agreed upon, the package designer develops the final layout and works with the production workers and product manager to produce the package.

REQUIREMENTS

High School

In high school, you should take classes in art and computers, including computer-aided design and graphics, if available. Technical classes such as electrical shop, machine shop, and mechanical drawing will also be helpful when working in the manufacturing industry. In addition to developing artistic abilities, you should also develop communication skills through English and writing classes. Foreign language skills are also beneficial.

Postsecondary Training

Educational requirements vary, but because competition in this field can be fierce, postsecondary education is highly recommended. Most entry-level design occupations require a bachelor's degree or a degree from a design school. Some positions as assistants to designers are available for those with training from two- and three-year design schools that award certificates or associate's degrees upon completion. The best option for career advancement is to attend an appropriate college or university to earn a bachelor's or master's degree in fine arts. Programs usually cover core subjects such as English, history, and the sciences, and include various art classes such as design, studio art, and art history. Other beneficial classes include computer-aided design, business administration, basic engineering, computerized design, mechanical drawing, psychology, sales, and marketing.

Other Requirements

If you are interested in packaging design, you should be highly creative, imaginative, have mechanical aptitude and manual dexterity, and verbal and visual communication skills. In addition, you will need analytical and problem-solving skills and should enjoy working with others because packaging designers often work in teams. You should be familiar with the use of computers in design and manufacturing and be able to work well under pressure.

EXPLORING

Pick one of your favorite products—such as a type of soda, a candy bar, or a video game—and redesign the packaging. How would you change the design to attract different demographic groups (such as kids or senior citizens)? Experiment with color and graphics to try to create something completely different than what you see.

To get a taste of what the job of packaging designer is like, talk to your high school counselor about arranging an interview with someone in the field. Think of some questions you might like to ask, such as how they prepared for the field, what got them interested in the work, and what they like best about their job. Chances are, their answers will be very enlightening to your own search.

While in high school, take as many art classes as you can and get involved in outside projects to further develop your skills. See if you can get some design experience through the theater department, designing costumes, stage sets, or even playbills. Getting involved in the arts is not only fun, but also can help you gain a sense of whether or not you enjoy design work.

EMPLOYERS

Various packaging and manufacturing industries employ packaging designers. Employment opportunities are also available with companies that contract out package design services. Package designers usually work with a team of employees and managers involved with the product to be packaged.

Packaging is one of the largest industries in the United States, so jobs are plentiful across the country. However, the field of graphic design is highly competitive because there are many talented people attracted to this career. Fortunately, there are many areas of employment for designers. In addition, many prefer to be self-employed as freelance designers.

Opportunities in the packaging field can be found in almost any company that produces and packages a product. Practically all products, such as food, chemicals, cosmetics, electronics, pharmaceuticals, automotive parts, hardware, and plastics, need to be packaged before reaching the consumer market. Because of this diverse industry, jobs are not restricted to any geographic location or plant size.

STARTING OUT

Students in a graphic arts program may be able to get job leads through their school's career services office. Many jobs in packaging are unadvertised and are discovered through contacts with professionals in the industry. Students may learn about openings from teachers, school administrators, and industry contacts they have acquired during training.

Applicants can also apply directly to machinery manufacturing companies or companies with packaging departments. Employment opportunities may also be available with design studios that specialize in packaging designs.

ADVANCEMENT

Packaging designers who work with a design firm usually begin in entry-level positions and work their way up as they gain design experience and build their portfolio. Packaging designers who work for a manufacturing company may advance within the department to become product manager, or may choose to move into corporate communications and marketing areas.

Some packaging designers pursue additional education to qualify as design engineers. Others may pursue business, economics, and finance degrees and use these additional skills in other areas of the manufacturing or design industries.

EARNINGS

Earnings for packaging designers vary with the skill level of the employee, the size of the company, and the type of industry. The U.S. Department of Labor reports that the median salary for graphic artists, which includes packaging designers, was approximately $42,400 a year in 2008. The lowest paid 10 percent earned $26,110, while the highest paid 10 percent earned $74,660 or more. A designer who has established an excellent reputation can earn considerably more. Benefits vary and depend upon the company, but generally include paid holidays, vacations, sick days, and medical and dental insurance. Some companies also offer tuition assistance programs, pension plans, profit sharing, and 401(k) plans. Designers who are freelancers usually have to provide their own insurance and savings plans.

WORK ENVIRONMENT

Packaging designers who work in a manufacturing setting usually work in a studio or office that is well lit and ventilated. However, they may be subjected to odors from glues, paint, and ink when paste-up procedures are used. Also, as computers are used more and more, designers are often sitting in front of a computer for a considerable amount of time.

Occasionally, they may have to be in a noisy factory floor environment when observing product packaging and production. Most plants are clean and well ventilated although actual conditions vary based on the type of product manufactured and packaged. Certain types of industries and manufacturing methods can pose special problems. For example, plants involved in paperboard and paper manufacturing may be very dusty from the use of paper fibers. Workers in food plants may be exposed to strong smells from processing. Pharmaceutical and electronic component plants may require special conditions to ensure that the environment is free from dirt, contamination, and static. Though these conditions may require some adjustment, in general, most plants have no unusual hazards.

Most designers work 40 hours a week, although overtime may be required for the introduction of a new product line or during other busy manufacturing periods.

OUTLOOK

According to the *Occupational Outlook Handbook,* employment of all designers is predicted to grow about as fast as the average for all careers through 2018. Opportunities will be good for packaging designers as businesses will always need talented workers to develop appealing packaging design concepts. However, there is tough competition for the jobs available. Individuals with little or no formal education and limited experience may find it difficult to find a job.

Because packaging is one of the largest industries in the United States, jobs can be found across the country, in small towns and large cities, in small companies or multiplant international corporations. In addition, jobs are not restricted to any one industry or geographical location.

FOR MORE INFORMATION

For information on graphic design careers, contact the following organizations:

American Institute of Graphic Arts
164 Fifth Avenue
New York, NY 10010-5901
Tel: 212-807-1990
http://www.aiga.org

Industrial Designers Society of America
45195 Business Court, Suite 250
Dulles, VA 20166-6717
Tel: 703-707-6000
http://www.idsa.org

For information on accredited design schools, contact

National Association of Schools of Art and Design
11250 Roger Bacon Drive, Suite 21
Reston, VA 20190-5248
Tel: 703-437-0700
E-mail: info@arts-accredit.org
http://nasad.arts-accredit.org

Photo Stylists

QUICK FACTS

School Subjects
Art
Business

Personal Skills
Artistic
Communication/ideas

Work Environment
Indoors and outdoors
Primarily multiple locations

Minimum Education Level
Some postsecondary training

Salary Range
$64 to $350 to $800+ per
day

Certification or Licensing
None available

Outlook
About as fast as the average

DOT
N/A

GOE
N/A

NOC
5243

O*NET-SOC
N/A

OVERVIEW

Photo styling is actually an all-encompassing term for the many and varied contributions that a *photo stylist* brings to the job. Primarily, the photo stylist works with a photographer to create a particular image, using props, backgrounds, accessories, clothing, costumes, food, linens, and other set elements. Much of the work exists within the print advertising industry, although stylists are also called to do film and commercial shoots. There are many specialties that can be included on a photo stylist's resume, from fashion to food, bridal to bathrooms, hair and makeup styling, to prop shopping and location searches. Some stylists may focus on one specialty; others may seek to maintain a wide repertoire of skills. While photo styling may seem like a vague and nebulous profession, it is an increasingly vital part of the photography and advertising industries.

HISTORY

Photo styling has existed since the first photographs were taken. Someone, whether it is a photographer, an assistant, a studio worker, a designer, or an editor, has to make sure all the elements within the frame are arranged in a certain way. Hair and makeup stylists in the film and publishing industries were probably the first to gain recognition (and credit). In fact, most people still associate "styling" exclusively with hair and makeup work, without fully appreciating the contribution of other stylists to the finished photo or film. To this day, photo styling credits are only occasionally listed in fashion and advertising spreads, but that trend is changing. Society is becoming more visually oriented, and the contributions made by stylists are becoming more important. Stylists are gaining the respect of people within the film, television, and print industries. Some photographer/stylist teams are as well known for their collaborative work as are actors and directors. After toiling in relative obscurity for many years, photo stylists are emerging as powerful voices in industry and in society.

THE JOB

The photo stylist is a creative collaborator, working with photographers, art directors, models, design houses, and clients to produce a visual image, usually for commercial purposes. It is both a technical and artistic occupation. The kind of work a photo stylist performs depends upon, among other things, the nature of the photography; the needs of the photographer, studio, and art director; and the requests of the client. Because these factors vary from one situation to another, it is impossible to list all the aspects of a photo stylist's job. In simple terms, what a stylist does is help to create a "look." The specifics of how it is done are far more complicated. Moreover, "photo styling" itself is a very general term—there are many kinds of styling, almost as many as there are reasons for taking a photograph.

Prop gathering and set decoration are the most common assignments in photo styling, but there are many subspecialties within the field, each requiring different skills and experience. For example, fashion, wardrobe, and portrait shoots often require a number of professional stylists on hand to scout locations, prepare the set, acquire clothes and accessories, dress the models, and style hair and makeup.

The following paragraphs provide more information on specialties in the field.

Food stylists employ a variety of techniques, such as painting and glazing, to make everything from a bowl of cereal to a crawfish etouffee appear especially appetizing.

Home furnishings and domestic items specialists often introduce various props to give a natural look to the photographic set.

On-figure stylists fit clothes to a model, and *off-figure stylists* arrange clothes in attractive stacks or against an interesting background.

Soft-goods stylists introduce appropriate fabric, linens, and clothing into a shoot. The *tabletop stylist* may use anything from glue to Vaseline to give an added allure to a set of socket wrenches.

Hair and makeup stylists are almost invariably cosmetic specialists, and are usually present on any set that employs live models.

Casting stylists locate modeling talent. Other stylists specialize in set design, child photography, bedding, bridal, and catalogs. Many stylists are adept in more than one area, making them difficult to categorize.

Stylists may also bring special talents to the set, like floral design, gift wrapping, model building, or antiquing. They usually have a "bag of tricks" that will solve problems or create certain effects; a stylist's work kit might include everything from duct tape and cotton wadding to C-clamps and saltshakers. Sometimes a photo stylist is called upon to design and build props, perform on-set, last-minute tailoring, even coordinate the entire production from the location search to crew accommodations. The most successful stylists will adapt to the needs of the job, and if they can't produce something themselves, they will know in an instant how and where to find someone who can. Versatility and flexibility are key attributes no matter what the stylist's specialty.

Being prepared for every possible situation is a large part of the photo stylist's job. Knowledge of photographic techniques, especially lighting, lenses, and filters, can help a stylist communicate better with the photographer. An understanding of the advertising industry and familiarity with specific product lines and designers are also good tools for working with clients.

Organization is another vital aspect of the photo stylist's job. Before the shoot, the stylist must be sure that everything needed has been found and will arrive on time at the studio or location. During the shoot, even while working on a model or set, the stylist must be sure that all borrowed materials are being treated with care and that preparations for the next shot are underway. Afterward, he or she must return items and maintain receipts and records, so as to keep the project within budget. The freelance stylist does all this while also rounding up new assignments and maintaining a current portfolio.

Only part of the stylist's time is spent in photo studios or on location. Much of the work is done on the phone and on the street, preparing for the job by gathering props and materials, procuring clothes, contacting models, or renting furniture. For the freelancer, lining up future employment can be a job in itself. A senior stylist working in-house at a magazine may have additional editorial duties, including working with art directors to introduce concepts and compose advertising narratives.

Even during downtime, the stylist must keep an eye out for ways to enhance his or her marketability. The chance discovery of a new boutique or specialty shop on the way to the grocery store can provide the stylist with a valuable new resource for later assignments.

Maintaining a personal directory of resources is as essential as keeping a portfolio. Staying abreast of current trends and tastes through the media is also important, especially in the areas of fashion and lifestyle.

What a stylist does on the job depends largely upon his or her unique talents and abilities. Photo stylists with the most experience and creative resources will make the greatest contribution to a project. As a premier stylist, that contribution extends beyond the set to the society as a whole: shaping its tastes, making its images, and creating art that defines the era.

REQUIREMENTS

High School

There are a number of classes you can take to help prepare you for this career while you are still in high school. Take classes in the visual arts to learn about design and composition. Develop your hand–eye coordination in sculpture or pottery classes. Painting classes will teach you about colors, and photography classes will give you a familiarity using this medium. Skill with fabric is a must, so take family and consumer science classes that concentrate on fabric work. You will be able to cultivate your skills pressing and steaming clothes, doing minor alterations, and completing needlework. Because your work as a photo stylist may require you to work as a freelancer (running your own business) take mathematics classes or business and accounting classes that will prepare you to keep your own financial records. Of course, English classes are important. English classes will give you the communication skills that you will need to work well with a variety of people, to promote your own work, and to drum up new business. The specialties employed for certain shoots require a familiarity with, for instance, food preparation, home decorating, children, formal attire, bedding, and any number of other potential subjects. A photo stylist, like any artist, draws from his or her own experience for inspiration, so exposure to a wide variety of experiences will benefit anyone entering the field.

Postsecondary Training

There is no specific postsecondary educational or training route you must take to enter this field. Some photo stylists have attended art schools, receiving degrees in photography. Others have entered the field by going into retail, working for large department stores, for example, to gain experience with advertising, marketing, and even product display. The Association of Stylists and Coordinators

(ASC) recommends entering the field by working as an assistant for an established stylist. According to the ASC, such an informal apprenticeship usually lasts about two years. By then, the assistant typically has enough skills and connections to begin working on his or her own.

If you are interested in a specialized type of styling, you may want to consider gaining experience in that area. For example, if hair and makeup styling interests you, consider taking classes at a local cosmetology school that will teach you how to work with different kinds of hair. If food styling interests you, consider taking cooking or baking classes at a culinary school. Again, this will give you experience working with the materials to be photographed. It is essential to have a knowledge of photography for this work, so continue to take photography classes to build your skills. Advertising courses may also be useful.

Other Requirements

The personal qualities most sought in a photo stylist are creativity, taste, resourcefulness, and good instincts. Stylists work with a variety of people, such as clients, models, and prop suppliers, and therefore they need to have a calm and supportive personality. Schedules can be hectic and work is not always done during normal business hours, so stylists need flexibility, the ability to work under pressure, and patience. Stylists who are easy to work with often find that they have a large number of clients. Finally, an eye for detail is a must. Stylists are responsible for making sure that everything appearing in a photo—from a model's hairstyle to the size and color of a lamp—is exactly right.

EXPLORING

There are a number of fun ways to explore your interest in this career. Try teaming up with a friend to conduct your own photo shoot. Arm yourself with a camera, decide on a location (inside or outside), gather some props or costumes, and take a series of photographs. At a professional level, these are known as test shots and are used to build up the portfolios of photographers, models, and stylists. But a backyard photo shoot can be a good way to appreciate the elements involved with this career. Obviously, any opportunity to visit a real photographer's set can be an invaluable learning experience; ask your counselor to help you arrange such a field trip. You should also consider joining a photography or art club. Besides giving you the opportunity to work with the medium, such clubs may also sponsor talks or meetings with professionals in the field.

Look for part-time or summer work in the retail field where you may have the opportunity to set up displays and learn about advertising. Even if you can't find such work, watch someone prepare a display in a department store window. Many stylists start out as window dressers or doing in-store display work.

EMPLOYERS

There are relatively few positions available for full-time, salaried photo stylists. Some ad agencies, magazines, and companies that sell their merchandise through catalogs have stylists on staff. Most photo stylists, however, work as freelancers. They are hired for individual assignments by photographers, ad agencies, design firms, catalog houses, and any other enterprise that uses photographic services.

STARTING OUT

A person can enter the field of photo styling at any point in life, but there is no clear-cut way to go about it. Some people, if they have the resources, hire photographers to shoot a portfolio with them, then shop it around to production houses and other photographers. However, most prospective employers prefer that a stylist have previous on-set experience.

As the ASC recommends, one of the best ways to break into this field is to find work as a stylist's assistant. Production houses and photo studios that employ full-time stylists usually keep a directory of assistants. Most cities have a creative directory of established stylists who may need assistants. It is important to always leave a name and number; they may have no work available immediately, but might be desperate for help next month. Working as an assistant will provide you with important on-set experience as well as show you the nuts and bolts of the job—including the drudgery along with the rewards. Building a reputation is the most important thing to do at any stage of this career, since most photographers find stylists by word of mouth and recommendations, in addition to reviewing portfolios. Assistants will also be introduced to the people who may hire them down the road as full-fledged stylists, giving them an opportunity to make a good impression. Eventually, you can seek out a photographer who needs a stylist and work together on test shots. Once you have enough examples of your work for a portfolio, you can show it to agents, editors, and photographers.

Agency representation can be of enormous help to the freelancer. An agent finds work for the stylist and pays him or her on a regular basis (after extracting an average commission of 20 percent).

The benefit of representation is that while a stylist is working one job, the agent is lining up the next. Some agencies represent stylists exclusively; others also handle models, photographers, and actors.

ADVANCEMENT

Advancement in this field can be measured by the amount of bookings a stylist obtains, the steadiness of work, and a regularly increasing pay rate. It can also be determined by the quality of a stylist's clients, the reputation of the photographer, and the nature of the assignments. Some stylists start out with lower-end catalogs and work their way up. If the goal is to do high fashion, then the steps along the way will be readily apparent in the quality of the merchandise and the size of the client. The opportunity to work with highly regarded photographers is also a step up, even if the stylist's pay rate remains the same. In a career built on reputation, experience with the industry's major players is priceless. Senior stylists at magazines often help in ad design and planning. Some stylists advance to become art directors and fashion editors. Ultimately, each stylist has his or her own goals in sight. The "rare-air" of high fashion and celebrity photography may not be the end-all for all stylists; a good steady income and the chance to work regularly with friendly, creative people may, in fact, be of more importance to a stylist.

EARNINGS

Like almost everything else in this field, earning potential varies from one stylist to the next. Salaries at production houses can start as low as $8 an hour, but usually include fringe benefits like health insurance, not to mention a regular paycheck. The freelancer, on the other hand, has enormous earning potential. An experienced fashion or food stylist can demand as much as $800 or more a day, depending on his or her reputation and the budget of the production. Regular bookings at this level, along with travel and accommodation costs (almost always paid for), translate into a substantial income.

Most photo stylists, however, earn less and average approximately $350 to $500 per day. According to the ASC, assistant stylists, who are hired by the day, can expect to make approximately $150 to $200 per day. Neither assistants nor stylists who are freelancers receive any kind of benefits. They must provide for their own health insurance and retirement, and they receive no pay for sick days or vacation days. In addition, while a stylist may have a job that pays $500 a day for several days, the stylist may also have unpaid periods when he or she is looking for the next assignment.

WORK ENVIRONMENT

Work conditions for a photo stylist are as varied as the job itself. Preparation for a shoot may involve hours on the telephone, calling from the home or office, and more hours shopping for props and materials to use on the set. Much of the work is done inside comfortable photo studios or at other indoor locations, but sometimes, especially in fashion and catalog photography, outdoor locations are also used. If the merchandise is of a seasonal nature, this could mean long days working in a cold field photographing winter parkas against a snowy background, or it could mean flying down to Key West in January for a week shooting next summer's line of swimwear. Travel, both local and long distance, is part of the job. Days can be long, from dawn to dusk, or they may require the stylist's presence for only a few hours on the set. Hours vary, but a stylist must always be flexible, especially the freelancer who may be called in on a day's notice.

Regardless of whether stylists own or rent photo and prop equipment, they must be prepared to put out a lot of their own money. Most clients and studios budget for these expenses and reimburse the stylist, but the initial funds must sometimes come from the stylist's own pocket. Maintaining a portfolio, purchasing equipment, and paying agents' fees may also add to the cost of doing business.

Photo styling can be an extremely lucrative career, but there is no assurance that a stylist will find steady employment. It is wise to establish an emergency fund in the event that work disappears for a time. Busy periods often correspond to seasonal advertising campaigns and film work. A stylist might have a great year followed by a disappointing one. Freelancers must file their own quarterly tax returns and purchase their own health insurance.

Stress levels vary from one assignment to the next. Some shoots may go smoothly, others may have a crisis occur every minute. Stylists must be able to remain calm and resilient in the face of enormous pressure. Personality clashes may also occur despite every effort to avoid them, adding to the stress of the job. For the freelancer, the pressure to find new work and maintain proper business records are still further sources of stress. Photo stylists will also spend considerable time on their feet, stooping and kneeling in uncomfortable positions or trying to get something aligned just right. They also may need to transport heavy material and merchandise to and from the studio or location or move these elements around the set during the shoot. Reliable transportation is essential.

The irregular hours of a photo stylist can be an attraction for people who enjoy variety in their lives. Work conditions are not always that strenuous. The work can also be pleasant and fun, as the crew trades jokes and experiences, solves problems together, and shares the excitement of a sudden inspiration. The rewards of working with a team of professionals on an interesting, creative project is a condition of the job that most stylists treasure.

OUTLOOK

The value of a good photo stylist is becoming more and more apparent to photographers and advertising clients. However, the outlook for employment for stylists depends a great deal on their perseverance and reputation. Larger cities are the most fertile places to find work, but there are photo studios in nearly every community. The fortunes of the stylist are intrinsically related to the health of the advertising, film, video, and commercial photography industries. Stylists should try to maintain a wide client base, if possible, so they can be assured of regular work in case one source dries up.

Technological advances, especially in the areas of digital photography and photo enhancement, may transform, but not eliminate, the role of the photo stylist in the future. Someday there may be educational avenues for the stylist to enter into the field, and this may increase the amount of competition for styling assignments. Ultimately, though, maintaining the quality of work is the best insurance for continued employment.

FOR MORE INFORMATION

For information on the career of photo stylist, contact
Association of Stylists and Coordinators
18 East 18th Street, #5E
New York, NY 10003-1933
E-mail: info@stylistsasc.com
http://www.stylistsasc.com

To see examples of professional photography and read about news in the field, check out the following publication and Web site:
Photo District News
770 Broadway, 7th Floor
New York, NY 10003-9522
Tel: 646-654-5780
http://www.pdn-pix.com

Production Designers and Art Directors

OVERVIEW

Production designers are responsible for the overall look of the visual elements and approve the props, costumes, and locations in films, videos, music videos, and television commercials. *Art directors* are the top assistants of production designers; they ensure that the production designer's vision is implemented.

HISTORY

Art directors and production designers have been in demand ever since the first film was made and the television industry emerged in the 1950s. In fact, the first Academy Award for excellence in the field of art direction (known then as interior decoration) was awarded in 1928. Art directors and production designers continue to play a key role in establishing the visual look of movies, television shows, music videos, and commercials.

In the past, the title "art director" was used to denote the head of the art department (hence the Academy Award for Best Art Direction). Today, production designers lead art departments with art directors serving as top assistants.

THE JOB

Production designers are responsible for all visual aspects of on-screen productions. In film and video and broadcast advertising, the production designer has a wide variety of responsibilities and often interacts with an enormous number of creative professionals. Work-

A production designer for a television series works on new designs in his studio. *(Beatrice Larco, AP Photo)*

ing with directors, producers, and other professionals, production designers interpret scripts and create or select settings in order to visually convey the story or the message. The production designer oversees and channels the talents of set decorators and designers, model makers, location managers, propmasters, construction coordinators, and special effects people. In addition, production designers work with writers, unit production managers, cinematographers, costume designers, and postproduction staff, including editors and employees responsible for scoring and titles. The production designer is ultimately responsible for all visual aspects of the finished product.

The director may hire a *storyboard artist* to illustrate his or her ideas for camera moves and editing of complicated scenes or sometimes the entire film. A few directors will draw a storyboard themselves or use a software program such as Frame Forge 3D.

Preproduction on a film is designed to be the most efficient use of time and money. The time budgeted for set design and construction is tight and with a set deadline there is constant revision and planning to complete the sets on time for the scenic painters and decorators to complete their contributions and have them ready for shooting.

Production designers supervise the project from preproduction through production with the assistance of *art directors*. Art directors are the top assistants of production designers. They must have both creative and management skills to ensure that the production designer's vision is being implemented. They are responsible for the entire operation of the production division or just particular departments such as construction, props, locations, special effects, and set dressing.

REQUIREMENTS

High School

There are a variety of high school courses that will provide both a taste of college-level offerings and an idea of the skills necessary for success on the job. These courses include art, drawing, art history, graphic design, illustration, photography, shop, and desktop publishing.

Other useful courses that you should take in high school include business, computing, drama, English, technical drawing, cultural studies, psychology, and social science.

Postsecondary Training

A college degree is usually a requirement for production designers and art directors; however, in some instances, it is not absolutely necessary. Courses in art direction, production design, photography, filmmaking, set direction, advertising, marketing, layout, desktop publishing, and fashion are also important for those interested in entering this field.

Because of the rapidly increasing use of computers in design work, it is essential to have a thorough understanding of how computer art and layout programs work. For smaller productions, the production designer or art director may be responsible for using these software programs; for larger films, a staff person, under the direction of the designer or director, may use these programs.

Other Requirements

The work of production designers and art directors requires creativity, imagination, curiosity, and a sense of adventure. They must be able to work with all sorts of tools and building materials; use specialized equipment and computer software, such as graphic design programs; and be able to communicate the ideas behind their work.

Other requirements for production designers and art directors include time-management, communication, and organizational skills, as well as the ability to see the "big picture."

EXPLORING

Read books and magazines about the field. Here is one book suggestion: *The Art Direction Handbook for Film,* by Michael Rizzo (St. Louis, Mo.: Focal Press, 2005). Watch as many movies, television shows, and commercials as possible to learn more about the visual elements that make these creative offerings interesting to viewers. Ask your drama teacher or counselor to arrange an interview with a production designer or art director.

EMPLOYERS

Typical employers include film and television production houses, movie studios, Web designers, multimedia developers, computer games developers, and television stations. Other employers include advertising agencies, publishing houses, museums, packaging firms, photography studios, marketing and public relations firms, desktop publishing outfits, digital prepress houses, or printing companies.

STARTING OUT

The positions of production designer and art director are not entry level. Typically, a person on a career track toward the position of production designer or art director is hired as an assistant to an established professional.

Serving as an intern is a good way to get experience and develop skills. Graduates should also consider taking an entry-level job at a film or television studio or production company or in a publisher's art department to gain initial experience. Either way, aspiring production designers and art directors must be willing to acquire their credentials by working on various projects.

ADVANCEMENT

While some may be content upon reaching the position of production designer to remain there, many production designers take on even more responsibility within their organizations, become film or television directors, start their own design agencies, or pursue production design opportunities outside the film and television industries. Many people who get to the position of production designer do not advance beyond the title but move on to work on more prestigious films or television shows or at better-known production companies. Competition for top positions continues to be strong because of the large number of talented people interested in entering these careers.

Art directors advance by becoming production designers, by working on more prestigious projects, and by working for larger companies.

EARNINGS

The weekly base pay for a motion picture art director who is a member of the International Alliance of Theatrical Stage Employees is approximately $3,000, but top production designers can negotiate higher salaries of more than $10,000 per week. Production designers who work on nonunion productions typically have lower earnings. Annual earnings for production designers and art directors may range from less than $20,000 to more than $200,000 for experienced professionals.

According to the U.S. Bureau of Labor Statistics, earnings for salaried set and exhibit designers and art directors ranged from less than $25,150 to more than $154,840, with median earnings of $44,660 to $76,980 in 2008.

Film companies employing production designers and art directors pay into the Art Directors Guild's Health & Pension Fund. Production designers and art directors who are members of the International Alliance of Theatrical Stage Employees or National Association of Broadcast Employees and Technicians receive health insurance and a pension as part of their membership benefits. Freelance nonunion production designers and art directors employed in the motion picture and television industries are usually responsible for providing their own health insurance and other benefits.

WORK ENVIRONMENT

Production designers and art directors often work under pressure of a deadline and yet must remain calm and pleasant when dealing with coworkers. They must work as many hours as required—usually many more than 40 per week—in order to finish projects according to predetermined schedules. They work on set in comfortable conditions, but also frequently travel to film sets that can be located throughout the world in a wide variety of settings.

OUTLOOK

The U.S. Department of Labor predicts that employment for production designers and art directors who work in the film and television industries will grow faster than the average for all careers through 2018. These professionals play a major role in the look of a film and, as a result, will continue to be in steady demand in coming years. However, it is important to note that there are more production designers and art directors than the number of available job openings. As a result, those wishing to enter the field will encounter keen competition for salaried, staff positions as well as for freelance work.

FOR MORE INFORMATION

The guild is a local union of the International Alliance of Theatrical Stage Employees, Moving Picture Technicians, Artists and Allied Crafts of the United States, Its Territories and Canada. Contact it for information on art directors who are employed in the moving picture industry.

Art Directors Guild & Scenic, Title,
    and Graphic Artists Local 800
11969 Ventura Boulevard, 2nd Floor
Studio City, CA 91604-2619
Tel: 818-762-9995
http://www.artdirectors.org

This union counts film and television production workers among its craft members. Visit its Web site for information on education and training.

International Alliance of Theatrical Stage Employees, Moving
    Picture Technicians, Artists and Allied Crafts of the United
    States, Its Territories and Canada
1430 Broadway, 20th Floor
New York, NY 10018-3348
Tel: 212-730-1770
http://www.iatse-intl.org

This union represents scenic and production designers, art directors, and other professionals working in film, television, industrial shows, theatre, opera, ballet, commercials, and exhibitions.

United Scenic Artists Local 829
29 West 38th Street, 15th Floor
New York, NY 10018-5504
Tel: 212-581-0300
http://www.usa829.org

Toy and Game Designers

OVERVIEW

Toy and game designers develop and create a variety of entertainment products, from stuffed animals and action figures to video games and virtual pets. While these creative specialists often determine the general design to be used, they usually work with a team of developers (including editors, illustrators, production managers, and play-testers) to manufacture a product for an intended audience.

Classified as *industrial designers,* toy and game designers work primarily for publishers, development firms, software firms, and manufacturing companies. Most designers work as freelancers; there are probably no more than a few thousand full-time professionals employed in the United States.

HISTORY

Children have always learned through play. As a result, toys and games have existed, in one form or another, since the dawn of civilization. In the Stone Age, rattles were made from gourds and musical instruments from bones. Wooden sleds, used by hunters to transport food, date back to 6500 B.C. Toys and games have also been discovered in Roman, Greek, and Egyptian burial sites and among the remains of the Aztec and Mayan cultures. Many Germans were skilled at carving wooden toys in the Middle Ages, with each family member often developing a particular carving specialty.

While toy artisans and craft workers had been practicing their craft for centuries, they didn't receive any kind of formal recognition

QUICK FACTS

School Subjects
Art
English

Personal Skills
Artistic
Communication/ideas

Work Environment
Primarily indoors
Primarily one location

Minimum Education Level
Bachelor's degree

Salary Range
$31,400 to $57,350 to $98,370+

Certification or Licensing
None available

Outlook
About as fast as the average

DOT
142

GOE
01.04.02

NOC
2252

O*NET-SOC
27-1021.00, 15-1099.13

until the Renaissance. Although the toys and games of that period were relatively simple compared to those that we know today, the introduction of automatic and mechanical toys created a sense of wonder among the people of the time.

The toymaking industry formally emerged in Germany, with the town of Nuremburg serving as a distribution center for local toymakers. By the end of the 1700s, toy sellers and designers were able to reach large numbers of customers through the use of catalogs.

In the United States, colonial period toys were made from scraps of cloth, wood, and even corncobs. Many of the designs for these folk toys were passed from one generation to the next. Throughout the 1700s, Americans continued to create homemade toys and games. In the late 1830s, William Tower organized a guild of toymakers in Massachusetts. A decade later, the American toy and game industry was born.

Many early toys and games were produced by designers and artists working in tool manufacturing or cabinetmaking, making these entertainment products on the side. It wasn't until after World War II that the toy and game industry grew big enough to support full-time professional designers.

Today, toy and game designers create everything from interactive dolls to role-playing video games. Advanced technology combined with the growing use of computers and the Internet will give designers of the future unlimited opportunities to create unforgettable products for children and adults alike.

THE JOB

Whether they are self-employed or work on staff, most toy and game designers have similar duties and responsibilities. In general, designers are charged with creating the primary design of a new toy or game or for changing an existing product. In addition, designers must present ideas to management and/or clients, write up design documents describing every step required in creating a product, and work with either staff or outside sources to complete a project.

The first step in developing any design is to determine the needs of the client. In the toy and game industry, client needs focus not only on the physical product but also on safety issues (especially items intended for children under the age of three), the cost of the design, the age-appropriateness of the product, and marketplace competition.

Once designers have clearly defined their clients' needs, they usually conduct research on product use, materials, and production methods needed to create an appealing and competitive product.

They also must make sure that the item, or a similar one, is not already in existence. According to the Toy Industry Association, approximately 7,000 new products are introduced every year. With so many new products flooding the market, originality is essential in order for a new toy or game to catch the customer's eye and drive sales.

With all the research completed, the designer is ready to create a prototype (a mockup, sketch, computer-aided control drawing, or plan drawn to scale) to present for client or management approval. Prototypes often are quite detailed so that clients can easily understand how the finished toy or game will actually look and operate. Indeed, much of a designer's work involves the communication of ideas to clients, management, coworkers, and others.

After the general design has been approved, designers work with other team members or outside professionals to develop the actual product. In addition to graphic designers, illustrators, and production personnel, designers usually interact with or oversee the activities of developers, editors, playtesters, marketing specialists, and engineers as a toy or game goes through the various production stages.

Along with creative and artistic work, designers do a lot of writing. For example, they are usually responsible for writing the first draft of game rules or product instructions. Designers also have to write explanations of complex design concepts and the goals of a toy or game.

In addition to all of the responsibilities described, *independent toy and game designers,* also known as *independent inventors,* face other challenges. They must determine from the start, for example, whether they will sell their ideas to toy manufacturers (or have a broker sell the ideas for them) or manufacture and distribute their products themselves.

Self-employed designers who opt to sell their products or ideas must find a publisher or manufacturer and a distributor once the toy or game has been designed. Most companies seeking new products from outside sources purchase them from design firms and from independent inventors and agents with whom they already have an established business relationship. Milton Bradley and Hasbro, for example, prefer to work only with designers they know.

For this reason, independent designers may have a hard time penetrating the industry at the start of their careers. However, some major companies, having been forced to reduce their research and development departments because of economic pressures, are now turning to outside professionals more than ever. Games, in particular, are increasingly being designed by freelancers and then developed in-house by large toy manufacturers. In addition, independent designers may find opportunities at small- and medium-sized firms, which often are more receptive to the ideas of freelancers than larger companies.

Designers who decide to publish their own games or manufacture their own toys are, in effect, starting their own businesses. They need to either contribute a considerable sum of their own money to their start-ups or find investors. In addition, these designers must to be able to contract for production services at reasonable prices, track orders from retailers, ensure the timely delivery of all ordered products, and create promotional materials that stir customer interest.

As is true for all start-up businesses, proper planning is vital. Independent designers need to create a business plan, develop product ideas, project sales, and determine the most cost-effective ways to manufacture, distribute, and market their products. They also must attend trade shows, make sure that accounts are billed, and keep accurate records. To protect their invention, these self-employed designers must obtain a patent or trademark, especially if they hope to sell their products to a manufacturer or publisher once they have met with success in the marketplace.

Ultimately, designers who think that they want to start their own toy or game companies must realize that most of their time will be spent running their businesses, not designing products. They should also be aware that about 90 percent of all new businesses fail in the

Major Toy and Computer Game Companies

- Activision (http://www.activision.com)
- ALEX (http://www.alextoys.com)
- Atari (http://www.atari.com)
- Disney (http://www.disneystore.com)
- Electronic Arts (http://www.ea.com)
- Fisher-Price (http://www.fisher-price.com)
- Hasbro (http://www.hasbro.com)
- The LEGO Group (http://www.lego.com)
- Mattel (http://www.mattel.com)
- Nintendo (http://www.nintendo.com)
- SEGA (http://www.sega.com)
- Spin Master (http://www.spinmaster.com)
- Toys R Us (http://www.toysrus.com)

first two years. On the other hand, many hugely successful toys and games, such as Monopoly, Uno, and Scrabble were designed and marketed by independent, inspired inventors.

REQUIREMENTS
High School
While in high school, you can take a variety of classes to prepare for more advanced courses offered at colleges and universities. In the creative arena, take various art and design classes. Other recommended courses are animation, creative writing, photography, filmmaking, music, and theater.

While art courses are important for aspiring toy and game designers, a solid liberal arts background is invaluable. Therefore, you should study a variety of subjects, including math, anthropology, computer science, public speaking, history, and literature. Classes that emphasize writing are especially vital, since designers must be able to communicate complicated design ideas to coworkers and clients alike.

Postsecondary Training
In general, most toy and game designers must have a bachelor's degree, even for entry-level positions. By earning a bachelor's degree in either industrial design or fine arts at a four-year college or university, you will be exposed to a variety of courses that will help you land an entry-level job and rise up through the ranks as a designer. Classes include art and art history, designing and sketching, principles of design, and other specialized studies. Liberal arts and business courses, such as merchandising, business administration, marketing, and psychology, will also prove to be invaluable. Take specialized courses in areas of particular interest to you. For example, if you're thinking about becoming a video game designer, game design, game programming, and related classes will be helpful.

While many colleges and universities across the nation and abroad offer excellent programs in industrial design and fine arts, some institutions provide specialized curricula geared especially to toy and game designers. The Fashion Institute of Technology in New York, for example, allows students to earn a bachelor of fine arts degree in toy design. In addition, the International Game Developers Association provides a list of schools located around the world for students interested in video game design. (See the end of this article for contact information.)

Other Requirements
In addition to being creative and imaginative, you also need to be able to communicate ideas, both visually and verbally, and be able

to work independently and as part of a development team. While motivation and perseverance are essential for success in the industry, it is equally important to be able to solve problems, be open to the ideas of others, and see beyond your own personal preferences in order to create what customers want.

Whether you work for yourself or for a company, self-discipline is vital. Both independent and staff designers must be able to initiate their own projects, budget their time wisely, and meet deadlines and production schedules. In addition to having business sense and sales ability, staff and freelance designers must stay on top of new products and developments in the field.

EXPLORING

If you are thinking about becoming a toy or game designer, there are many ways that you can investigate the field. Attend an industry show to keep abreast of the latest products and to meet toy and game developers, publishers, and manufacturers. The American International Toy Fair, the biggest toy trade show in the United States, showcases toy and entertainment products from approximately 1,200 manufacturers, distributors, importers, and sales agents around the world.

Subscribing to industry-related publications can give you a sense of what is expected of toy and game designers, as well as where the market is heading. In addition to its regular issues, *Playthings* magazine (http://www.playthings.com) publishes a special *Buyers Guide,* which contains material geared especially for designers and inventors.

To gain some hands-on experience, you may want to join a "virtual company" whose members design games at low or no cost in their spare time. Volunteer to help at a variety of Web sites that focus on toys and gaming. Although toy and game firms usually hire professionals as *playtesters* (individuals hired to test new products), contact manufacturers to see if they are looking for in-house or off-site volunteers.

Getting to know designers working in toys and games can serve as a handy resource and contact. As mentors, they can help you break into the field by introducing you to employers and manufacturers and provide guidance once you have landed your first job.

EMPLOYERS

Unlike workers in other industries, most toy and game designers are self-employed. Many create toys and games on a part-time basis in addition to working other jobs. Alternatively, some designers who opt to develop their own toys or publish their own games actually create their own businesses, handling all operational aspects required, from idea conception to marketing and production.

Full-time toy and game designers are employed primarily by publishers, development firms, and manufacturing companies. While most industrial designers work for consulting firms or large corporations, toy and game designers can find job opportunities at every kind of toy company, from small start-ups to the industry giants, such as Hasbro, Milton Bradley, and Mattel.

STARTING OUT

Without experience, aspiring toy and game designers usually begin as *design assistants*. Assistants handle much of the background work needed for developing products. Through this work, assistants can learn more about the toy and game market so that, in time, they can become lead designers. Large firms are more likely than smaller companies to hire assistants, who usually have little or no experience.

If a design opportunity is not available, you may want to consider a related position as a production assistant or playtester. Many designers actually get their jobs only after working in other positions in the industry.

Employers looking to hire designers often contact local universities or industry associations. In addition, many place ads in local newspapers in search of qualified candidates. Regardless of how you make your initial move into the field, be sure to develop a portfolio of your design work and familiarize yourself with the products and future plans of potential employers.

Provided you have the necessary capital, it is relatively easy to enter the industry as a start-up; toy and game companies frequently purchase ideas after they have been made successful. On the other hand, larger firms usually do not accept new product ideas from independent inventors. These companies find it more cost-effective to employ staff designers than to pay royalties to freelancers.

ADVANCEMENT

Although it is virtually impossible to find an entry-level job as a toy or game designer, people with ambition and potential can find many opportunities to get into the industry and then rise through the ranks. A variety of junior positions, such as those in playtesting or customer service, can springboard qualified people into assistant designing jobs. After several years of experience, capable assistants at large companies, guided and nurtured by senior or lead designers, can then become toy and game designers themselves.

Once a designer penetrates the toy and game industry, there are various advancement paths possible. A creative director at Hasbro, for example, began as a production assistant. From there she went on to become a graphic designer, a senior designer, the assistant art director, and, finally, the creative director.

While most people in the industry opt to work either for a company or for themselves, some staff designers decide to leave their salaried positions and start their own businesses. Others become department heads, industry executives, or agents who negotiate the sale of ideas to various toy and game companies.

EARNINGS

In general, toy and game designers earn approximately as much as industrial designers in other specialty fields. The U.S. Department of Labor reports that the median salary of commercial and industrial designers was $57,350 in 2008. The lowest paid 10 percent earned $31,400 or less, while the highest paid 10 percent earned $97,770 or more.

Game Developer magazine reports that game designers had average salaries of approximately $67,379 in 2008. Game designers with less than three years of experience earned approximately $46,208. Those with three to six years' experience averaged $54,716 annually, and those with more than six years' experience averaged $74,688 per year. Lead designers/creative directors earned higher salaries, ranging from $60,833 for those with three to six years' experience to $98,370 for workers with six or more years of experience in the field. It is important to note that these salaries are averages, and some designers (especially those at the beginning stages of their careers) earn less than these amounts. These figures, however, provide a useful guide for the range of earnings available.

Unlike independent designers, professionals on staff often receive a variety of benefits in addition to their salaries, depending on the organization for which they work. These benefits may include health and life insurance, paid vacation and sick days, and pension plans.

WORK ENVIRONMENT

The environment in which toy and game designers work varies, depending on the employer. Manufacturing firms and design companies usually provide designers with well-lit, comfortable offices or other workspaces. These design professionals generally work a regular 40-hour workweek, although overtime is occasionally required in order to complete projects by designated deadlines. Self-employed designers often work longer hours, especially when they are establishing themselves in the industry.

Both staff and freelance designers frequently schedule their days in order to accommodate clients. It is not unusual for a design specialist to meet with a client in the evenings or on weekends, for example. Such meetings may take place in the designer's office, at the client's home or place of business, or at other locations, such as manufacturing plants or showrooms.

Toy and game designers work with other professionals, including editors, illustrators, graphic designers, playtesters, and production workers. The abilities to communicate and to get along with others are, therefore, imperative. In addition, many designers must work under pressure in order to please clients and finish projects on time. Finally, while most designers feel a sense of satisfaction and pride from developing creative ideas and products, some occasionally feel frustrated when their designs are rejected or substantially changed.

OUTLOOK

According to the *Occupational Outlook Handbook*, employment opportunities for all commercial and industrial designers are expected to grow about as fast as the average through 2018. Demand for toy and game designing professionals in particular will result from continued emphasis on the quality and safety of products, as well as on toys and games that are easy to understand and appropriate for their intended audiences. Increasing global competition will also play a role in the demand for toy and game designers.

Emerging technologies will continue to positively impact the employment outlook for design professionals as well. Those designers who have knowledge of and experience with high-tech toys, electronic versions of board games, and interactive video games will definitely have a competitive edge in the job market.

Children today are often more tech-savvy than their parents; toy companies need to cater their designs to meet the younger generations' increasing demand for high-technology products.

Although employment growth is expected, the U.S. Department of Labor notes that all designers will face intense competition for available job openings. Since many talented designers are attracted to the toy and game industry, those without formal design education, creativity, and perseverance will have trouble establishing careers in the field. Independent designers will also continue to have difficulty penetrating the industry. On the upside, many job openings will be available for qualified designers as demand continues and as designers leave the field for a variety of reasons.

FOR MORE INFORMATION

For information on obtaining a bachelor's degree in toy design, contact
Fashion Institute of Technology
227 West 27th Street
New York, NY 10001-5992
Tel: 212-217-7999
E-mail: FITinfo@fitsuny.edu
http://www.fitnyc.edu

For career information, contact
Industrial Designers Society of America
45195 Business Court, Suite 250
Dulles, VA 20166-6717
Tel: 703-707-6000
http://www.idsa.org

For information on industry issues, education options, and scholarship opportunities, contact the following organizations:
International Council of Toy Industries
Permanent Secretariat
c/o Toy Industry Association
1115 Broadway, Suite 400
New York, NY 10010-3466
Tel.: 212-675-1141
E-mail: info@toy-icti.org
http://www.toy-icti.org

International Game Developers Association
19 Mantua Road
Mt. Royal, NJ 08061-1006
Tel: 856-423-2990
http://www.igda.org

For industry information and other resources aimed at both kids and parents, contact
Toy Industry Association Inc.
1115 Broadway, Suite 400
New York, NY 10010-3466

Tel: 212-675-1141
E-mail: info@toyassociation.org
http://www.toy-tia.org

For information on industry news, purchasing a subscription, and its annual Buyers Guide, *contact*
Playthings Magazine
http://www.playthings.com

Index

Entries and page numbers in **bold** indicate major treatment of a topic.

D

E